Weekly Meditations: 2011-2014

Weekly Meditations: 2011-2014

Daniel R. Heischman

 National Association of Episcopal Schools
Excellence Through Association

National Association
of Episcopal Schools
815 Second Avenue
New York, NY 10017

National Association of Episcopal Schools, New York 10017
© 2016 by the National Association of Episcopal Schools.
All rights reserved.
Printed in the United States of America.

ISBN 1-58777-046-6

Cover photo by Chen Heng Kong/shutterstock.com.

Contents

xi | Foreword
Edmund K. Sherrill II

2011-2012
3 | Time to Reflect?
5 | Ready to Serve
7 | Is Failure Making a Comeback?
9 | Be Careful Out There!
11 | What's Really Important!
15 | Homecoming
17 | The Power of Kindness
19 | Absolutely!
21 | All Souls
23 | The Second Beginning
25 | What's in the Bucket?
27 | Thoughts on a Cyber Monday
29 | Daring to Be Prescriptive
31 | Finding Your God

Contents

33	The Uses of Disenchantment
35	A Model of Aloneness
37	A School's Presence
39	Voice and Pitch
41	Why We Do What We Do
43	What Were They Thinking?
45	Are You Serious?
47	The Search for Safety
49	A Welcome and a Framework
51	The Aftermaths of Tragedy
53	The Glue That Holds Us Together
55	Sacred Tensions
57	God's Time and Our Time
59	The "Where" of Resurrection
61	God's Inclusiveness
63	Calling All Introverts!
65	Springtime Challenges
67	Springtime Challenges II
69	Setting Limits
71	The Privilege of Service
73	Shedding Light

2012-2013

77	Returning to School!
79	In Praise of Awe
81	The Hidden Dimensions of Episcopal Identity
83	Back-to-School Nights and Days
85	Loving What Is Mortal
87	Changing Our Minds and Hearts
89	Cheating: Bad News and Good News
91	The Humming Chorus

93	Identity and Identities
95	The Two-Eyed Life
97	Sure Indicators
99	Two Worlds
101	Chaplain or Chaplin?
103	Because We Are...
105	Words with Practices Attached
107	Waking Up to Advent
109	Shop, Shop, Shop!
111	Beyond Words
113	Holy Dialogue
115	Second Thoughts on Multitasking
117	The Uncomfortable Goal
119	Communication of Integrity
121	Those "Other Religious Schools"
123	Ash Wednesday's Dilemma
125	No Escape!
127	A Comeback for Moderation?
129	The Answer Is Local
131	The Perfect Storm
133	Blessings
135	The Many Sides of Celebration
137	Knowing When It's Time
139	Rediscovering Etiquette
141	Something in Common
143	Being at Table
145	The Great Irony
147	The Weariness Factor
149	Whit Monday
151	The Year in Stone

Contents

2013-2014

155	Why We Come Back
157	Side By Side
159	Rising to the Occasion
161	Be Not Anxious!
163	On Being an Adult, Part One
165	On Being an Adult, Part Two
167	The Trophied Life
169	God Is with Us
171	Leaning Hard on "Episcopal"
173	Crisis to Crisis?
175	Taking It Personally
177	The Heart of the Matter
179	The Return of Laughter
181	The Goldilocks Zone
183	Thank God, We're Free
185	Unintended Consequences
187	Advent Advice
189	Finding God in Unlikely Places
191	The Other End of Resolutions
193	Facing Cold Winds
195	Out of Character
197	Hope for the Future
199	Underrated Forms of Communication
201	On the Front Lines
203	Where's the Bible?
205	Recalling Our Goals
207	What's Next?
209	Ash Wednesday Controversies
211	The Look
213	A Sign of Permanence

215	Getting the Soul Out of Bed
217	It Can Wait
219	Going Deeper
221	Like the Very First Time
223	Skeptics and Cynics
225	Consideration
227	Communities of Trust
229	Being Watched
231	The End of Vacation?
235	About Daniel R. Heischman

Foreword

Begun in September 2011, the Weekly Meditation is a regular email from the Reverend Daniel R. Heischman, executive director of the National Association of Episcopal Schools, to the Association's member heads, rectors, and chaplains. Oftentimes, they are forwarded to greater constituencies within school communities. The message is intended to inspire and encourage us as we guide and tend to our institutions and the students and families in our care. It is something I, and my colleagues, eagerly await each Monday morning during the school year. NAES is delighted and, in fact, honored to publish these pieces from this endeavor's first three school years (2011-2014) in this volume, making them available to the wider school community and The Episcopal Church.

Heads of school and trustees; vestry members and parish clergy; bishops and diocesan staff; faculty members, chaplains, and administrators; parents; educators in general: All will find Dan's pithy and thoughtful musings about the rhythm and culture of our schools, their Episcopal identity, the demands of leadership, and the education and moral development of our students to be honest, accurate, and uplifting. Whether you read them singly, or explore a month's or year's worth of messages in one sitting, you will find yourself, by turns, comforted, provoked, encouraged, and nourished for your journey both within and through Episcopal schools.

As we prepare our students for living faithfully and well in the twenty-first century, may this collection renew our energies for reflection, and strengthen our commitment to the ideals of godly service and care for others that lie at the heart of our Episcopal schools.

The Reverend Edmund K. Sherrill II
Governing Board President
National Association of Episcopal Schools
May 2016

2011-2012

Time to Reflect?

September 12, 2011

When I went to the local ATM machine this morning, I was met with a surprising message from the default page on the screen. "Time to Reflect," it read, referring, of course, to the 10th anniversary of September 11th. On the one hand, I was pleased that the folks at the bank were thinking about the tragic event that we recall with particular intensity this week. It was a nice, even poignant change of pace from the normal commercial greeting one receives on such screens!

At the same time, I thought it was a telling example of the way in which our culture can jump from one thing to the next, what we might refer to as our particular brand of cultural attention deficit disorder. Now it is time to "do reflection," for a brief period; then quickly we will be on to other things! As if we can stop amidst all of the rush of our lives and quickly shift gears!

It made me think about the value of what we do, day after day, in Episcopal schools. We all know that we cannot force our students to be reflective, with a simple change of pace. It takes time, and it takes a context where the invitation to reflect is always present. That is why we do chapel on a regular basis—we cannot expect all of our students to take advantage of it every day, but over the long haul, in a cumulative fashion, we make time for reflection to occur, when the time is right and our hearts are ready.

What makes our "time to reflect" distinctive is the fact that the invitation is always there, and we support that invitation by providing a place and ethos that actually encourages the reflection that we all need to engage in, not to mention that our culture desperately needs.

Ready to Serve

September 19, 2011

There is a new and important feature of the website for Episcopal Relief and Development (ERD). It is called "Ready to Serve," and it is intended to be a place where one can sign up as an individual who is ready and willing to serve in case of a disaster in one's own region of the country. ERD is compiling this new database of potential volunteers in light of what has been a spring and summer full of natural disasters on our very doorsteps, in our own hometowns, and in the most unlikely of places.

To me, the idea of readiness makes very good sense from the standpoint of the need for widespread volunteer support, particularly given what we may be coming to expect as an increase in the sheer volume of these unexpected and unwelcome events, perhaps as a result of the changes in our climate.

Readiness is also, I believe, a very apt image of what we are trying to do in Episcopal schools, to instill and cultivate a readiness to serve. With the velocity of change only likely to increase, with uncertainty being our constant companion and adaptability a necessity for any leader, the future may require of us as much of a readiness as a possession of any given skill. The quality of our character and the depth of our faith may be best seen in how we respond to unexpected situations. To respond in such a way that reflects our core strengths and convictions, a calmness and generosity of spirit, and an alertness to the workings of God in the most unlikely of places, requires a readiness.

One could define that readiness in many ways, but our times require, above all, an ability to enter into uncertainty, in essence a readiness to be unready. How often, in the reporting of natural disasters around our country, have we heard local citizens say, "I've never seen it like this before?" This readiness is not just a preparation for the unexpected, but a willingness to enter into the mystery of unanswerable questions and never-seen-before experiences.

Fortunately, Episcopal schools are places that value both a sense of service as well as a sense of mystery. What better combination can there be to cultivate the readiness for what lies ahead of us?

Is Failure Making a Comeback?

September 26, 2011

In July of this year, an article appeared in *Atlantic Monthly* ("How to Land Your Kid in Therapy," by Lori Gottleib) in which the writer claimed that the "cult of self-esteem," including the desire to rescue our children from unhappy experiences, was not equipping young people for the tasks of adulthood. Drawing upon the sources of many writers in the field, she concluded that, in shielding them from discomfort, failure, and struggle, we are actually making it harder for our children to grow up. Then, this past week's *New York Times Magazine* carried an article about how students' future success and happiness may depend more on their experience with failure and setbacks than the avoidance of them ("The Character Test," by Paul Tough, September 18, 2011).

Both of these articles have been read with great interest and already have prompted a good deal of conversation. Perhaps one of the questions emerging from these discussions might be, "Are we beginning to reacquaint ourselves with the educative value of failure?" As Mark Roosevelt, the new president of the revived Antioch College, remarks (a few pages later, in another article in this issue of the *New York Times Magazine*), "Our teachers need to tell students, 'Trying and failing is OK.'"

It is probably too early to know, in a culture that has been quite averse to the educative value of failure, whether or not we are collectively ready to reverse course and embrace failure's place in the development of young people. To my way of thinking, it is probably going to take more than the simple conclusions, "It is good for them," or, "It builds character," to stem the tide.

It will need something that—at the risk of sounding smug— Episcopal schools possess, namely, a theological context in which failure is seen and experienced as the beginning of new life. From our theological perspective, this is part of God's pattern of redemption. We may not look forward to it, nor see its value when experiencing it, but our tradition provides the undergirding theological framework that allows failure to take its rightful place in the experiences of life and help give meaning to life.

As the prayer for young people, in the Book of Common Prayer, puts it, "Help them [young people] take failure, not as a measure of their worth, but as a chance for new start."

I would say that is a pretty sound foundation upon which to greet whatever comeback failure may be making!

Be Careful Out There!

October 3, 2011

As many of you know, I spend a lot of time in airplanes. Last week I was onboard a plane served by an unusually perky and talkative flight attendant, one who sought—not altogether successfully—to be humorous, inspirational, and unconventional. As we landed, and it came time for her to sign off, she left us with the following admonition:

> Have an awesome Tuesday; have a fierce rest of the week; and, most importantly, be very, very careful out there.

A strange combination, I thought. On the one hand, she seemed to exhort us to take risks, say yes to life, be proactive, hit the ground running, or whatever metaphor you might draw upon to capture the spirit of embracing the tasks of life. At the same time, she urged great caution. It felt like a mixed message, to be sure!

Trying to be bold yet staying cautious. This is one of the strange and paradoxical symptoms of our culture. On the one hand, we are told to "go for it;" on the other hand, we know that the world can be unsafe, unpredictable, and misleading in its allure, "so be careful out there!" This combination is also reflected in our school communities: how many mission statements speak of the desire for students to take risks and, at the same time, how many of our families value, above all, the safety that we represent to them and provide for them?

It is a tension we need to consider and understand (albeit not resolve) better. This February, at our annual conference for chaplains and teachers of religion (ChapToR, as we call it), we will be considering the theme, "Fear and Faithfulness: Ministering to Communities in Transition." (February 15–17, 2012, in Austin, Texas). With the guidance of Professor Scott Bader-Saye, Professor of Ethics at the Seminary of the Southwest (and author of the book, *Following Jesus in a Culture of Fear*), we will be thinking a great deal about this tension between risk and safety, as those who minister in our schools juggle the gospel imperative to lose our lives while working with the cultural craving for a place of safety, something so many of our schools represent.

In the end, it may be that our students only begin to take risks when they feel safe, be that physical, emotional, or moral safety. Perhaps the flight attendant might have reversed the order of her parting words: "Be careful, and then have a fierce week!"

What's Really Important!

October 10, 2011

Thank you all for the very positive responses we have received for the Monday morning meditation from NAES. I suspect that, on occasion, you would welcome a different voice in this venue, and I am pleased to share, with her permission, a piece that Cindy LaPorte, head of school at All Saints' Episcopal Day School in Austin, Texas did in her September school newsletter. It was done in the aftermath of the terrible fires that hit Texas in late August and early September, fires that came very close to her own home.

DRH

Head Lines • September 2011

It's Sunday of the Labor Day weekend and although the wind is finally blowing from the north and the temperature is cooler than it has been in months, I am more uncomfortable than I have been in a long time. There is the sound of helicopters in the distance, smoke is swirling past the clouds, and the distinctive smell of burning brush fills the air. At dusk it is difficult to determine whether the orange glow in the west is from the setting sun or from the wildfire burning six miles away. And the question becomes, what should we do? Should we prepare to leave and if so, what should we take? I look around and try to determine what I have that can't be replaced.

Surely the original paintings and illustrations that my husband Jerry has done and the family photographs that decorate our walls must be among the first things that we will take with us. Or perhaps my collection of hearts or Jerry's collection of box wood rulers will be placed in the vehicle first. But then my mind races to things that belonged to my parents and grandparents: embroidered pillowcases and tablecloths; china that was too special to use; hand written family recipes; and the maple butcher block that my great-grandfather and grandfather used. Weary from worry, we go to bed.

I am awakened periodically by the flags on the porch wiping in the wind and the chimes in the trees playing what sounds like "Amazing Grace." Before I can slide out of bed to check on things, Jerry moves closer and wraps his arms around me. The dogs rush over from their beds and wiggle their noses under our covers. And I know then that there is no need to fill the car with stuff. As long as I am surrounded by those most dear to me and have the memories of those whose love I still miss, I know that I will be fine. People and pets and my camera to record new adventures will be what I take with me.

My prayer for us at the beginning of this new school year is that we will help each other to keep things in perspective. And that we will remember the words of author Patrick Overton:

> When you come to the edge of all the light you have, and must take a step into the darkness of the unknown, believe that one of two things will happen. Either there will be something solid for you to stand on—or you will be taught how to fly.

   The rest of the story: Late Monday afternoon the fire closest to us went from 80% contained to 40% contained. The residents of the neighborhood 5 minutes away were told that it was mandatory to evacuate. Although we were told we didn't have to leave yet, we were told that we should be prepared to do so. If we received a mandatory evacuation call, we would have 5 minutes to vacate the property. And despite what I wrote earlier in the day, it was just too difficult to not load a few of the things that I treasure most. Thankfully, the call never came.

Homecoming

October 17, 2011

We are entering what we might call the "Homecoming Season" for so many of our schools. For some, this is the time of the year when events are held that welcome alumni/ae and/or parents to the campus, thereby helping to strengthen the ties that bind our school to the larger world and to other generations of students.

For all schools, there is another type of homecoming that begins to make its rounds this time of the year. It represents, you might say, the, "End of the beginning," as Churchill put it, namely, the time in the school year when the excitement and the newness of the year give way to the reality of the school year, with all of its demands and occasional tensions. This, you might say, is a true, "Coming home," in that we have settled into the routine and now face the challenges and inevitables that routine poses to and for us. As one school head put it, "This is the time of the year when the true problems of the year begin to surface and settle in." Truly, home is a place of welcome and of new starts, but home is also a place of reality, where one's limitations and struggles are only too well known.

As the Zen saying goes, "After enlightenment, the laundry." Once the luster of returning has faded, we get down to the business of home, so to speak, including the realities of living in a community. The challenge for all of us is to hold on to the conviction that this—the laundry!—is as important and essential to God's agenda for a community as the excitement of new beginnings.

The Power of Kindness

October 24, 2011

Grant, O Lord, that in all of the joys of life, we may never forget to be kind.

– From the St. Paul's School Prayer

This past summer I presided at a memorial service for a man who had graduated from St. Paul's School in New Hampshire. As I was working on the service with the members of his family, each one spoke of how important the St. Paul's School prayer was for this man, and how its reference to kindness always brought tears to his eyes. They also spoke of how, on each important family occasion, he would bring out a copy of the prayer for all of the family to read together. Not only was it something deeply meaningful to him, but something he felt needed to be shared with those who meant the most to him.

It made me think about the cumulative impact and power of the prayers and rituals of our school chapel. I recall, for example, a woman in tears as I concluded a prayer offered in a church service; when I asked her if she was all right, following the service, she told me that the prayer I read was her own school's prayer, and how hearing it again had touched her so deeply. These words and practices have a way of shaping our souls and framing our deepest convictions. Perhaps for this St. Paul's graduate the experiences and chapters of his life had led him to believe, all the more deeply, in the power of kindness. Kindness may well have turned out for him to be far more than something "nice" relegated to the idealism of a school prayer. I suspect he had found it to be an active and dynamic force that fosters integrity, encourages empathy, and builds up the common life. He had, in essence, met up with the words of his school prayer in the lessons of his life.

A few weeks later I found myself sitting in a preschool chapel, thousands of miles away from New Hampshire. The chaplain at the preschool spoke to the children that day about the importance of practicing kindness. Suddenly I was struck by the power of such words being repeated and such values being emphasized, over time, not only in one school but in all of our schools, wherever they may be and whatever age range they may include. We are at our best as individuals when we are truly kind; we are at our best as a community of schools when we speak and pray, in common and repeated voice, about these powerful forces in our lives.

Absolutely!

October 31, 2011

A few weeks ago I listened to a fascinating and compelling speaker who addressed the many and profound changes that are upon us in schools. Learning has been democratized, he told us, the teacher is no longer the one who dispenses knowledge, and the classroom of the future will be tailor-made to meet the needs of each individual student—all true and ground-breaking realities. A new age has dawned, he told us, and he seemed to relish the role of heralding this new revolution. At the same time, I began to notice how often he used the word, "Absolutely," be it in response to questions asked from the audience, or in response to rhetorical questions he asked of himself. Curious about his use of this word, I started keeping count, and in one hour's time he had used the word at least fifteen times! Along with the dawning of this new era of change and flux, we were regularly hearing a word that evoked stability and constancy.

It reminded me of something that Bob Johansen, of the Institute for the Future in Palo Alto, California, observes in his book *Get There Early*. He notes the intensified use of this very word in our culture today, and attributes it to our deep need for clarity. "Absolutely," along with such words as, "exactly," and, "precisely," help us, in a confusing and complex world, get a sense of momentary control and comfort in a world of few absolutes. They give the speaker a sense of authority and finality, and their use in daily discourse is likely to increase in the future. It confirms the fact that, in a world where uncertainties are on the rise, there will be an accompanying and accelerated demand for clarity, even when that clarity is wrong.

I would go one step further: the increasing use of such words speaks to the deep human drive to seek an absolute, be it in a clear-cut or a highly confusing world. Heralds of dramatic change who gravitate toward such words remind us that we not only seek clarity, we seek a source and guide above all of that which confounds us, to which we can return and in whom we can trust. Whether we are aware of it or not, the "absolutelys" point to that basic human yearning for a divine purpose.

How fortunate we are, in Episcopal schools, to have the freedom to speak of an Absolute, in a world of "absolutely's." It will not furnish us with clarity on all matters, and it will not take away the uncertainties or the challenges to adjust to rapid change. But it will give us perspective, hope, and an understanding of what human beings, at root, are so desperately searching for in this world.

All Souls

November 7, 2011

Last week I traveled to Canada to conduct a retreat for the school chaplains of the Anglican Diocese of Toronto. The retreat was held in one of my favorite places of quiet, prayer, and a sense of the beloved community, the Convent of St. John the Divine, in Toronto. I arrived at the Convent in time for the midday Eucharist, on All Souls' Day (November 2nd). It was for the sisters of the community, as well as for all of us who observe All Saints' and All Souls' Days, a time to remember loved ones who have departed.

The preacher at the All Souls' service, the Reverend Nicola Skinner, spoke about the fact that in so many ways our relationships with those close to us have the potential for enrichment and completion beyond the time of their deaths. At the very least, they hold the potential of helping us realize how incomplete or unresolved some of those relationships were in this life. That alone, she reminded us, is redemptive.

I recalled, at that point, some words that a faculty colleague spoke to me in the aftermath of my father's death. "I talk more with my dad now that he is dead than when he was alive," he observed. By "talking," he meant sharing observations, asking questions, and raising unresolved issues about life or about their relationship. Those words were both comforting to me as well as hopeful, in that he was able to remind me there was room for my relationship with my father to continue and deepen in the years ahead without him on earth.

The preacher went on to say that, throughout the Old Testament God prefaces a lot of what God says by proclaiming, "I am the God of Abraham, Isaac, and Jacob." Note that God does not say, "I was the God…," but, "I (still) am…." Those relationships continue, shaping us and defining us, long beyond the end of their earthly span.

Our schools are places of life, potential, hope, and youthful exuberance. They can also be places of loss and grief, in so many possible different forms. The promise of our faith—that death is not the last word—is a true blessing for us as we help members of our community deal with the loss of a loved one. It also helps point the way as those who grieve begin to do what Rilke called the "heart work" with the ones we have lost, be it in the conversations we carry on with them, the deliberations we engage in about them, or in their words and actions that keep coming back to us, all things that continue to matter long after they have passed from us.

The Second Beginning

November 14, 2011

Mark Mullin was headmaster of St. Albans School during the first few years I was the head of upper school there, and I learned a great deal from working with him. In the autumn of my first year as division head, I had to address the students on a very difficult issue, something I was not looking forward to doing and certainly did not feel confident undertaking. To be sure, I was troubled that I had to address the issue at all—"Is this what being upper school head is all about?" I asked myself. When I had completed my remarks to the students, Mark took me aside, and said, "You have been in this job for over four months, but today you truly became the head of upper school."

As I review all of the positions I have held in the school world, I see in each two beginnings—the first was when I officially took the position, the second was when I truly became, as Mark put it that day, the person holding that position. What's more, in each of those situations the second beginning almost always had to do with facing up to a difficult situation. In some cases I felt I addressed the difficult situation adequately, in other situations I felt I did not; in all cases the opportunity to grow into the role and exercise true leadership came not through producing a happy outcome but through facing up to what simply had to be done, regardless of the effect.

How curious, that while we are likely to point to our accomplishments when we review our time in a particular position, what truly defines and shapes us are the challenging and difficult situations that God so often puts in front of us. I would venture to say that we are who we are, in our professional roles, more by virtue of the tough situations we face than by virtue of the successes we may point to with understandable pride. That is the lesson—indeed the blessing—of the second beginning!

What's in the Bucket?

November 21, 2011

You may know the story that Harry Mathews, former chaplain and retired school head, tells about a visit he made to Fiji. During that visit, he spent some time in a small village that was located on the banks of a swiftly-flowing and debris-filled river. While standing on the edge of that river one day, he saw a young boy on the opposite bank who proceeded to walk into the rapidly moving water, carrying a heavy tin bucket. Slowly, carefully, the boy slipped into the river, all of the time holding the bucket he was carrying above the water line. As the boy made his way across the river, Harry Mathews was struck by two things: first, the energy and courage it took to keep holding that bucket above the water; and second, he kept wondering to himself, what was in the bucket that was so precious? What contents were so valuable that the child would risk his own safety to keep them unharmed?

Later, Mathews would discover the contents of the bucket—it was the boy's schoolbooks!

It may not be schoolbooks, but chances are that all of the people who come to our schools each day—students, faculty, staff, administrators, and parents—come in part because of something they find at school, each day, that would be worth preserving in the same fashion. Each one of us, I dare say, have some things we cherish about coming to school that we would hope to keep above the water line.

The things we would put in our respective buckets may differ greatly, but as we draw toward Thanksgiving we might pause and remember the potential contents, those things that give us hope, meaning, indeed a sense of life itself. In some cases it may well be the very things we take most for granted in the course of our busy lives.

What would go in your bucket this Thanksgiving? What needs to be remembered, held up above the waters, in thanks to God for the blessings they bring? They may not only be the things we regard as precious and worthy of preservation at all costs, they may also be the very things that help us navigate the dangerous waters we must travel each day.

I wish you a very Happy Thanksgiving!

Thoughts on a Cyber Monday

November 28, 2011

Before opening my eyes, I listened. The wind outside the bedroom window did not screech or howl through the trees, but was more than a rustle or whisper. Twenty knots out of the southwest, just as the man in the box had predicted. The last thing I do before going to bed each night is listen. And the first thing I do each morning upon waking is listen.

This past weekend I completed Linda Greenlaw's book, *The Lobster Chronicles*, in which she tells the story of her life as a lobster fisherman, off of the Maine coast, in what is normally and decidedly a man's world. Toward the end of the book she writes about her need to listen—first to the weather forecast from the "man in the box," then how that forecast is confirmed or not confirmed in the early morning indicators outside her bedroom window. Such listening is crucial, she reminds us, in the late fishing season—right about now—when it can be safe to go out into the waters or it can be very dangerous. All the more important, she maintains, in such a shoulder season to be listening carefully.

As we enter what is likely to be one of the busiest times of year for all of us, be it at school or at home (and from what we witnessed on Black Friday and are likely to learn from Cyber Monday, there is no hint of any downsizing of that busyness in our immediate futures), it might be helpful to remind ourselves of the importance of listening this time of the year. Be it the first thing we do in the morning, or the last at night, or somewhere in between, we would be doing ourselves and others a real favor by incorporating some of the Advent notions of listening—watching, being alert, waiting in anticipation, listening to the quiet cries for help—to help us navigate through the intense days ahead of us.

In the words of the preacher at the Advent 1 service I attended yesterday, this is both a very full season but also a very dangerous season—emotionally, financially, and socially. Anyone who works with people on any deep level knows how trying these upcoming days can be. How important it is in this potentially perilous season to be listening for not only the signs of danger but also the opportunities to break away from the commercial and frenetic grip this season can have upon us.

In the midst of all that lies ahead, is there a place, a space, for all of us, where we might experience a regular moment for listening? Can there be a part of us, ready and yearning for God to speak that is not at the mercy of the expectations of this season? Among the many challenges of the season, that may be the biggest.

Daring to Be Prescriptive

December 5, 2011

I have been struck by the extent and depth of the reaction to the death of Apple CEO, Steve Jobs. Some have heralded him as the "secular prophet," as one who brought a sense of magic and coolness to the world of the "geek." The satirical newspaper, *The Onion*, referred to him as, "The only person in America who knew what he was doing." Recent revelations about his personal life have only enhanced the public's fascination with his influence, as seen in the fact that we are still talking about him months following his death.

What most fascinates me about Jobs was the fact that he believed, and we accepted, that he had something to offer to the world that it needed, and in many cases did not know that it needed. In essence, he had a prescriptive view of the world: Jobs had the confidence, the ability, indeed the conviction to be able to convince the culture that he knew what that culture needed before it knew that. In a *New Yorker* article written shortly after Job's death, a writer tells of the moment when he went on the Apple website. There, staring in front of him, on the home page, was a picture of Steve Jobs, before he got sick. And, as the writer put it, "He looked like he wanted to tell me something, but I did not know what it was."

It may be a stretch to equate the life and vision of Steve Jobs with what we do in schools, but there is at least one commonality. Underlying our openness to students, our flexibility in working with a wide variety of learning styles and our ability to meet students wherever they may be in their cognitive and emotional journeys, is a fundamental conviction that we have something of genuine value to offer to our students. It may come as a result of our schooling in a subject matter, or of what we believe is in the best interests of our students, or simply by virtue of an accumulation of common sense and life experiences. Whatever it may be, we dare to hold on to a confidence—shaky as it may be at times—that what we are doing and offering is of inherent value to our students and their families. It is not simply a matter of what the educational consumer wants. Likewise, in our conviction that Episcopal schools are places where the spiritual life is taken seriously, we hold to the belief that there is a reservoir of God's spirit in each of us, whether we know it or not, that is worth our time and attention.

We may find ourselves in that great transition from being the "sage of the stage" to the "guide on the side." We may have to rely increasingly on what our stakeholders tell us that they are looking for in a school. None of these transitions, however, take away from the fact that we hold to a conviction that what we are doing is of inherent worth and good, even if the culture does not yet know it!

Finding Your God

December 12, 2011

Normally, I do not derive a great deal of inspiration from airline magazines, so you can imagine my surprise when, last week, I found myself deeply engrossed in an excerpt from Eric Weiner's latest book, *Man Seeks God*, featured in one such publication.* Weiner shares the story of the moment in his life when he had been taken to the emergency room at a local hospital and told that he must have surgery immediately. Not knowing what was the matter, Weiner was understandably and intensely distraught, something that a nurse who was drawing blood from him, prior to the surgery, could obviously detect. Weiner describes the moment: "She (the nurse) maneuvered close to my ear, and said, slowly and clearly, words I will never forget: 'Have you found your God yet?'"

Weiner describes this occasion as one where the words of that question stuck to him. Why would she be asking him such a question? Was he about to meet his maker? Did she know something that he did not know? The nurse did not answer his questions, simply gave him a wise and knowing look, leaving him with his thoughts.

Upon reflecting on that question, Weiner—himself an agnostic—found it neither mean-spirited nor judgmental. It did convey to him a personal concern, not to mention, in his words, "the quiet certainty of someone who has found her God." What's more, it was a question that Weiner came back to, once the crisis of his health had passed. It also struck me as a highly inviting question, encouraging Weiner to explore his own tradition, one that might be very different from the nurse's own. She posed the question, but did not seem to expect a specific or immediate answer.

We are at our best, in Episcopal schools, when we are able to pose such important questions to our students. These are questions full of compassion, yet also challenge, reflective of our deep convictions as adults who are aware of how we can influence our students. These are also questions that are highly respectful not only of where students find themselves, in their own particular development, but also of the traditions (or lack thereof) from which they come. These are questions our students can come back to, indeed draw upon in their own moments of crisis or decision, to be answered at their own speed.

This season of the year is rich with images of biblical characters seeking to find their God. It is also a season that can easily provoke the question of God, given the deep contrast our students can detect between the root meaning of the season and how it gets distorted in commercial ways. How we pose the question of whether or not our students are finding their God—in word, music, liturgy, and pastoral care—can have a deep, even lasting impact on them. It can be something to which they can return, long after the Advent and Christmas seasons pass.

*See, Eric Weiner, "An Honest Inquiry," *US Airways Magazine* (December 2011), 53–62.

The Uses of Disenchantment

January 9, 2012

In a recent article in the *Chronicle of Higher Education*, a professor of Comparative Literature at Penn State University spoke of how she was teaching the novel, *The Kite Runner*, by Khaled Hosseini, during the time of the recent and tragic unfolding of the pedophilia scandal at that university.* The novel, of course, deals with the moral tragedy of a boy who witnesses a brutal sexual assault on his friend and fails to protect him, and the parallels to what was unfolding on that very campus were both obvious and poignant. When Professor McClennen asked her class about how the novel might be instructive for what the Penn State community was experiencing, students were quick to express their feelings and give words to the myriad of unanswered questions they had at that moment.

Many students told of how they were experiencing a certain feeling of disenchantment over the downfall of someone who was such an idol to so many of them, Joe Paterno. How could he make such a mistake? As some described it, "...if Joe Paterno could make a mistake, where did that leave them?"

Today our culture gives us ample opportunities to experience disenchantment with our heroes. People who were thought to be above reproach are discovered to have made compromises, gone against their alleged values, and let down a great many people who looked up to them. You might say that disenchantment could well be one of the signature experiences of our time, as people are almost routinely thrown off their pedestals and no longer regarded as esteemed role models.

How easy it is for young people to grow cynical watching their idols fall. How tempting it is not to believe in anyone who might lead us, once we experience disenchantment with the behavior of those whom we admire and respect.

Yet here is the very place where Episcopal schools serve such an important purpose. We dare to talk about redemption, second chances, beginning all over again, in a world that is highly unforgiving. We can make use of moments of disenchantment in a way that few schools can, for we can view the falling of idols against the larger backdrop of what our tradition says about human nature. We can leave our students with something more than cynicism when they are disenchanted: we can talk about hope, repentance, and new life.

Fortunately, we are not empty-handed when disenchantment prevails. We can make use of it, indeed grow as a result of it.

---

*See, Sophia A. McClennen, "Teaching 'The Kite Runner' at Penn State," *The Chronicle of Higher Education* (December 2, 2011), B20.

A Model of Aloneness

January 16, 2012

The minister at the church I attended as a child happened to be a classmate of Dr. Martin Luther King, Jr., at Boston University School of Theology. I recall from his sermons his frequent mentioning of this fact; I think, in retrospect, it had less to do with name dropping than the portrayal of a controversial figure at this time (this was a small town in the Midwest in the early 1960s) in more human and accessible terms. He helped a skeptical congregation feel more connected to this man. Frequently, the minister would speak of King as a quiet, reflective young student, deeply committed to his studies and someone who spent a good deal of time to himself. Some of that aloneness may have had to do with his social marginalization at the time as a person of color. It may also have to do with the fact that while King had a very public life he was also a man who spent a good deal of time in prayer, study, and introspection. Perhaps King was already having glimpses of what was going to be demanded of him, and he was wise enough to know that such a calling demanded care, discernment of this calling, and time alone with God.

So often we think of Dr. King as the "man out front," be it leading a march, confronting people of power, or delivering a stirring speech. To be sure, the development of equal rights in this country would not have been the same had he not played such a public and openly prophetic role. But there is also another side of King—his commitment to prayer, solitude, and devoted study, to those moments when, in his own words, he had "been to the mountaintop." His public persona is balanced by a time alone in preparation, replenishment, and reflection. In this balance between public and private he clearly reflects the rhythm of Jesus' own life and ministry.

We celebrate our heroes so often in terms of what we see of them, "out front." It is the important and tangible expression of their power and influence. Dr. King also teaches us that public presence is balanced by time alone, indeed that these times of aloneness are essential for the demands of prophetic leadership. Our students need to hear of that necessary balance, a balance that they are fortunate to take advantage of themselves in Episcopal schools.

A School's Presence

January 23, 2012

Recently I read the results of a very interesting study done by two professors at Notre Dame Law School on the impact of a Catholic school's presence in urban neighborhoods.* Specifically, the professors studied the differing rates of crime in neighborhoods where a Catholic school remained, as compared with neighborhoods where—as increasingly and dramatically is the case in many urban areas—a Catholic school had been replaced by a charter school, all in the city of Chicago. Utilizing data collected from police statistics in various beats in Chicago, they found lower serious crime rates in those beats that had a Catholic school in operation than from those without one. The study also found that a charter school replacing a Catholic school does not "replicate Catholic schools' positive community benefits." A Catholic school, in their view, seems to help suppress crime in a way that a charter school does not.

I do not pretend to understand all of the nuances implied in this study, nor make any judgments about the value of charter schools as opposed to Catholic schools. The study does lead me to wonder about the clear but often unarticulated value of a religious school presence in any neighborhood. What is it about a religious school that might have that calming, perhaps clarifying effect, an effect that even some very fine charter schools do not have?

So, too, it makes me think about how important it is for us to consider our schools' presence in the community, wherever it may be. A good many of our schools have not had altogether harmonious relationships with their neighborhood—the scars many school heads bear from zoning meetings and neighborhood gatherings is testimony to that!—while other schools may point to a more harmonious, indeed pivotal relationship with their neighborhoods. Many of those schools that have been at odds with the surrounding neighborhood may also nonetheless play such a pivotal role. Regardless, there is such a thing as "school presence," I believe, in the community, and all of the members of our school communities—students, faculty, staff, administrators, parents—need to be reminded of that presence. Particularly in a culture that can be very suspicious of institutions, the care with which we are a presence in the community is increasingly important. Who knows! We may be more important to the neighborhood than we realize!

*Nicole Stelle Garnett and Margaret F. Brinig, "Catholic Schools, Charter Schools, and Urban Neighborhoods," *University of Chicago Law Review*, 79, no. 1 (2012).

Voice and Pitch

January 30, 2012

I am blessed to receive a large number of school magazines, alumni bulletins, and annual reports, on a daily basis, and I try hard to look through all of them. As much as one publication might seem to resemble another, there is always something unique and compelling that comes through about each school in all of those volumes that load up my "to read" pile!

In the most recent issue of the St. Timothy's School (Maryland) magazine,* an alum of the school, Maisie Houghton, talks about her recently published memoir, *Pitch Uncertain: A Mid-Century Middle Daughter Finds Her Voice*. In the interview, Ms. Houghton refers to the impact a girls' school, such as St. Timothy's, can have on young women, most importantly that it can model how women, "can be good at things on their own." She goes on to say that the larger purpose of her memoir is, "to share a sense of the greater concept of 'voice' with my readers." Then she adds an interesting twist on the concept of voice: "I am still working on finding my proper voice, my certain pitch. Am I too strident or too timid?"

Reading the interview, I was struck not only by her reference to voice, but also to pitch. Many independent schools speak of helping students find their voice, and that is a most worthy, indeed urgent goal. Ms. Houghton goes on, however, to speak of pitch—what I interpret to be the how of that voice: how it is expressed, how that voice connects or does not connect with others, how that voice can best be heard. While the reference to voice focuses largely on the self, the notion of pitch involves not only the speaker but the listener, and how the voice that speaks can connect with those who are hearing this voice.

This distinction strikes me as an important example of what we are trying to do with students in Episcopal schools, at all ages and grade levels. We seek not only to help them find their voice, but discover a pitch that honors the listener. Voice may refer to self-expression, but pitch begins to touch on the quality and integrity of that voice, how it welcomes in others who will be privileged to hear that voice. Its focus on the how of speaking reminds us that the entire process, of which Ms. Houghton and all of our schools point to in valuing the finding of one's voice, ends up being an intensely ethical process. The alternative would be simply be a plethora of disconnected voices, with important words, in the words of the Bible, "falling to the ground" (I Sam. 3:19).

*See, "In Good Voice," *Verite Sans Peur* (St. Timothy's School, Autumn 2011), 17-21.

Why We Do What We Do

February 6, 2012

A couple of weeks ago I received a message from a colleague in California, sharing with me two emails she had received from parents, one right upon the other. The first elicited the reaction from her, "Why am I doing this?" The second, received minutes later, provoked a very different response, what she referred to as, "This is why I do what I do."

I think all of us can easily recall the contrasting responses, and in many cases they follow one right after the other. At our new heads program in September, Aimeclaire Roche, head of the Bishop's School in California, spoke of how the life of a school head can, "turn on a dime," enduring a difficult conversation in one moment, celebrating a joyous occasion the next. Moving so quickly from experience at the end of one spectrum to something almost exactly at the opposite, in virtually the next moment, was for her one of the most eye-opening experiences of being a school head.

As coupled as those contrasting situations can be for all of us, this time of year seems to hold more potential for the, "Why am I doing this?" type of experience. The walls can feel as if they are closing in, and it is a long stretch until spring vacation. We are juggling attention to the current academic year with increasing amounts of time devoted to next year. The idealism we carried with us back to school at the beginning of the academic year can seem a distant memory.

All the more important to remember what my colleague remarked when I wrote to her to ask if I could use her examples as a base for an upcoming Monday meditation. She replied that her big challenge—particularly perhaps this time of year?—is to seek out more of those "this is why I do this" reminders. After all, she tells us, we don't need to look far! They are there for the finding; we just need to be attuned to them!

What Were They Thinking?

February 13, 2012

Surely, this is the time of year when we can be easily frustrated by student behavior. Be it on an individual or group level, we can find ourselves repeating the words above, "What were they thinking?" Perhaps, we might wonder, was thinking actually part of the equation at all? We can find ourselves asking lots of basic questions regarding what students have done, perhaps what adults have done, as news of incidents reach our desks, and which may now require a corrective and appropriate response.

A cautionary note is always valuable. Our students, as well as the adults in our community, are fundamentally good people. We need to remind ourselves of this basic fact, over and over, as we meet unexpected and undesirable behavior at any level. Recently, the *New York Times Magazine* reported that, when it comes to surveys on teenage substance abuse and sexual behavior, our young people are actually more conservative than many of their parents.* While the internet and social media can open up new avenues of opportunity for us to wonder, "What were they thinking?" it can also allow for a more careful monitoring by parents of their children. As one school head recently wrote, in the aftermath of one of those large-scale incidents that can wreak havoc with the morale of a school this time of year, "We have a good school and good students." We should never lose sight of that simple reality in light of frustrating events.

These moments can also reacquaint us with another important perspective, something that strikes at the heart of what we are about as school communities. In our cultural push for young people to grow up faster, to acquire ever-greater intellectual skills and expose them to wider experiences, the cultivation of a moral compass is not automatic. Sophisticated, savvy, and very bright young people are not necessarily well-grounded in moral judgments. Indeed, as the Archbishop of Canterbury, Rowan Williams, wrote some years ago,** for moral judgment to flourish, young people need more, not less, time to grow up. The absence of that compass, which can come as a surprise to us, may well be an unwelcome and unintended consequence of our push to make students grow up before they are ready.

The crucial question might well be, in the words of the Archbishop, are we providing, for our children, "room to explore in safety, not to be prematurely committed?" It may well be the key ingredient in the cultivation of moral judgment, for what our students need to be thinking as they mature.

---

*See, Tara Parker-Pope, "The Kids Are More Than All Right," *The New York Times Magazine* (February 5, 2012), 14.

**See, "Childhood and Choice," in Rowan Williams, *Lost Icons: Reflections on Cultural Bereavement* (Edinburgh: T. & T. Clark, 2000).

Are You Serious?

February 20, 2012

The Reverend John Buchanan, longtime pastor of Fourth Presbyterian Church in Chicago, is retiring soon, and in a recent reflection on his 48 years of ministry, he told the story of one baptism he did for a two-year old. In accordance with Presbyterian tradition, Buchanan pronounced the child's name, followed by the declaration, "You are a child of God, sealed by the Spirit in your baptism, and you belong to Jesus Christ forever." The young child immediately responded, "Uh-oh!"

Buchanan thought that a very appropriate response, given the depth of the affirmation he had made on behalf of the child. So often we make our way through some profound and even stunning theological affirmations, in our worship, without stopping to consider just how serious these words and phrases can be in their temporal and eternal meaning. That is why we can count some of the challenging questions of some of our students to be such a gift, whatever their age, as they can remind us of the "uh-oh" dimension of what the tradition is saying, what we are saying. Are we serious in what we say, or simply just throwing out words and phrases? Do we embrace it all, part of it, or none of it?

Indeed, a common question that young people ask these days is, "Are you serious?" They ask it in routine ways of each other, they are asking it—directly or indirectly—of us as adults. Behind what seems to be a routine question is a much deeper one, reflecting what these young people are looking for in life. They want to know where the seriousness can be found. Do we really mean what we are saying and doing? That is an enormous challenge for us to face; we can count it both a daunting task and an immense blessing when they have the courage to ask it of us.

The Search for Safety

February 27, 2012

For all of our schools, the safety of our students—their physical safety, as well as their emotional and moral safety—is of primary concern. When it comes to judging between competing claims for the good, it trumps the others every time. At the same time, almost all of us, I am sure, have had to deal with requests from some parents to do things in the interest of safety that go beyond what we feel is reasonable and healthy in assuring the well-being of our students. As Aristotle might describe it, safety can easily become a virtue in excess!

We had a fascinating discussion on this matter at our annual ChapToR Conference (Chaplains and Teachers of Religion in Episcopal schools), last week in Austin, Texas. Professor Scott Bader-Saye, who teaches ethics at the Seminary of the Southwest, spoke about how our culture manufactures and cultivates fear, issuing in an all-consuming desire for safety in every corner of life. Safety sells, he reminded us, and part of its curious appeal is its ability to make us anxious about the questionable safety of virtually everything we do and encounter. Tell a story about new revelations challenging the safety of a toy or medication, and we stop and listen.

Professor Bader-Saye made one observation that has stuck with me. In the absence of a common understanding in our culture of what it means to be a good parent, as well as to raise good children, safety becomes the "default mode" in the process of assessing our parenting skills. If we are actively working, on all fronts, for the safety of our children, then we can assure ourselves that we are being a "good enough parent." All one needs to do is to look at recent surveys on why parents send their children to private and independent schools—in recent years safety has become the number one reason, outscoring academic strength or small classes—to understand some of what he is talking about.

As I think about this contemporary "benchmark" of good parenting, I also wonder how much of the search for safety is a disguised form of a deeper human yearning. St. Augustine said that our hearts are restless until we rest in God. If we find ourselves obsessing about safety, could it be that we are looking for something more than just a refuge from harm? Sometimes, after all, the soul can trick us: just when we thought we were clear about what we were looking for, it turns out that there is a deeper human search going on. Our wish, to others, that they, "Be safe," may in fact be a way of putting into words something we hope for at a much deeper level.

A Welcome and a Framework

March 5, 2012

At our recent retreat for chaplains and parish day school rectors in the Pacific Northwest, Bishop Hanley of Oregon made mention of a new, emerging trend, "home churching." Like home schooling, this phenomenon has its roots in a family's dissatisfaction with what institutions provide or do not provide, as well as an interest in offering some spiritual and moral framework for children whose parents are not particularly interested in church going, or perhaps seek to carve out their own approach given their varied religious or non-religious backgrounds. It also appears to have an organic beginning in most homes: what begins as a day of the week set apart without television or internet then gives way to grace before meals, Bible study, singing songs, family discussions, and planning for the week ahead. Before one knows it, a pattern and ritual have emerged. As some of these parents report, "Church really did not work for us," and this provides for them a spiritual alternative.

One of the ways that "church really did not work for us" is the discomfort these parents can feel having their children in church, including the seeming lack of welcome they can experience for bringing their children in the first place. When the children make noise, these parents claim to receive a lot of "nasty and disapproving looks" from the older folks around them in the pews.

I don't think the church does a particularly good job of addressing the expectations it has for the behavior of children in worship. On the one extreme, there are those churches where the nasty looks abound, where the implicit message to kids and the parents who bring them is, "Not welcome;" on the other hand, there are those churches where children can seem out of control, admittedly making it hard for many adults to focus on the liturgy. It encourages me when parishes intentionally seek to welcome children "as they are" in worship, although children—like all human beings!—need help with what is appropriate and inappropriate behavior, even in a sacred space. It is a struggle that many parishes face: how to blend welcome with needed guidelines.

Here is where I believe our Episcopal schools do such a good job with children and worship. Our chapels are welcoming places for children, where we center our message and tone to their world. At the same time, we help our students learn how to act in a sacred place. They are given a framework, something they all seek and need. In some cases, they ultimately have a better sense of how to be in a sacred place than their parents when they show up to chapel!

A welcome and a framework: the two go hand in hand when it comes to having that most important part of the Body of Christ in our midst. In this way, among many, we have something of real value to offer to our churches.

The Aftermaths of Tragedy

March 12, 2012

So many images fill my head and heart from the aftermath of last week's terrible news from Episcopal School of Jacksonville (ESJ), including the experience I had of being at the memorial service for Dale Regan at the school on Friday.

I recall the movement from watching the unfolding of events on Tuesday with our staff in the office, via the web, to the glorious service at the school on Friday, presided over by the Bishop of Florida, the Dean of the Cathedral in Jacksonville, and school chaplain, the Reverend Hopie Jernagan. Truly, there was a sense of resolution in that movement from media-splashed breaking news to the proclamation, at the memorial service, of resurrection.

I recall the faces of ESJ students at the memorial service: clearly, from their expressions, they had lost someone dear to them; I recall thinking about the faculty gathered there: all good faculties, as we know, think a lot about how they might have done things differently, and no doubt these fine people were asking the natural, lingering questions of how they might have missed something or done something differently; I thought about the many parents at the service, and how their worst fears for the safety of their children were touched by this event; I thought about the board members, who must have been wondering how do they now lead the school from this tragedy; I thought about the many school heads represented there, whose learning of the news of unwelcome events at another school is usually accompanied by the sobering recognition of how easily this might have happened on their own turf.

I thought about the countless expressions of support that came, the preceding days, from schools around the country. Truly, this particular school community was carried and surrounded by a wide community of prayer, a community made even more cohesive and apparent through the experience of supporting another school.

Then I recall the large number of clergy from the Diocese of Florida who had assembled at the service, giving their time and pastoral sensitivity to a place that meant something to them and very much needed their presence. Moreover, as the service began, I recall the message sent out from Bishop Sauls, Chief Operating Officer at the Episcopal Church Center in New York City, announcing that the chapel there would be available for those who wished to observe some moments of silence at the very time the memorial service began. Truly, from these and other expressions of pastoral presence and support, I recalled how blessed we are to have the larger company of the church connected to our schools.

Finally, I was reminded of something that comes to me often, but at no time more poignantly than during the liturgy on Friday: we share with all schools the potential human hurt and tragedy that can so easily come in life, yet we truly set ourselves apart in the manner in which we deal with that tragedy once it has occurred.

How blessed, I concluded, we are to be in Episcopal schools!

The Glue That Holds
Us Together

March 19, 2012

> More than any other firm on Wall Street, Goldman Sachs
> forged a set of shared values and beliefs.
>
> – Charles D. Ellis, *The Partnership:*
> *The Making of Goldman Sachs*

Wednesday's op-ed page of the *New York Times* featured a piece
that has caused quite a stir in the investment banking world.* An
employee of Goldman Sachs for twelve years wrote about why
he was leaving the firm that very day. In essence, it had to do
with what he observed as the change of culture at the firm. That
notion of culture, he maintained, was always a mainstay of the
way the firm worked: teamwork, integrity, humility, and doing
right by their clients. "This," he explained, "was the secret sauce
that made this place great." Now, he concluded, it is all about
making money, frequently at the expense of the client.

The reaction to the article has been strong and swift. Some
have maintained that these are the parting words of a disgrun-
tled employee; others speculate on how he ever got the idea that

there was any degree of "moral fiber" to this business in the first place. Others echo his concern about how things have changed, not only in the investment banking world but in so many other venues.

Culture, as defined in the book mentioned above, is, "the commitment to shared values," and, likewise, "the glue that holds the firm together." Proudly, we pay a good deal of attention in our schools to the culture of the community, and the shared values that serve as our respective glues. Regardless of the motivation and circumstances behind this particular challenge to an institution known for its attention to culture, the writer of this week's article does remind us of the perennial challenge when it comes to describing our school culture and promoting our core values: it is one thing to define them for the benefit of identity and marketing; it is another thing, on a regular basis, to check out with our community whether or not we are actually living out those values. If we do not engage in the latter activity, we may well find ourselves surprised one day to learn that the culture we thought was in place is no longer there!

*See, Greg Smith, "Why I am Leaving Goldman Sachs," *The New York Times* (March 14, 2012), A24. My thanks to Ann Mellow, Associate Director of NAES, for directing me to the article.

Sacred Tensions

March 26, 2012

A fascinating exchange of views recently took place on the pages and website of the *Portland Press Herald* (Maine). It had to do with the decision of some Episcopal churches in the Portland area to offer "Ashes on the Go," this past Ash Wednesday. These churches, and their clergy, determined that they needed to go to the people on that day, rather than expect people to come to them. Hence, they stood in the middle of Monument Square, in the heart of Portland, fully vested with urns of blessed ashes, and dispersed them to those who were hurrying by. This practice was also replicated in many other contexts throughout the country (one group labeled its outreach that day as, "Ash and Dash").

Initially, one writer criticized the action, saying that it was demeaning to and lowering the dignity of the Ash Wednesday liturgy. Something as solemn as Ash Wednesday should take place only within the confines of sacred space. This represented a commercialization of the holy day, disrespectful of the beginning of the Lenten season.

Others quickly responded to the critique. One who participated in the event spoke of the appreciation of many who stopped to receive ashes. "Oh, thank you," one was reported to say, "I forgot it was Ash Wednesday and I am too busy to go to church. You brought the church to me." Another spoke of how the church needs to get itself out of its stone edifices and go directly to the people: "Where are all of the Peters and Pauls who brought Jesus' message to the masses?" she asked.

This conversation is symbolic of the classic religious tension between preserving the sacred and extending it to connect with the practices and language of those we are trying to reach. It is surely reflected in the great challenge we face, in our schools, of engaging children and youth at the level of faith: do we meet them where they are, or do we seek to bring them to a different place? Will they show up if we expect them to come to us? Are we compromising belief by tailoring the message to contexts that are familiar to them? In the case of, "Ashes to Go," was this meaningful church outreach or a sanctioning of frenetic life styles?

Like all tensions, I suspect this is one we must live with, and that is not a bad thing. As long as both sides of the tension have a voice, then we may just be finding ourselves in the right place. My guess is that those giving out ashes on Monument Square returned to be a part of more solemn observances of Ash Wednesday, later that day. I would also guess that they felt deeply fulfilled by participating in both contexts.

God's Time and Our Time

April 2, 2012

I've been reviewing a curriculum on financial literacy for middle school students, put out by the Seifert Foundation, and I was struck in looking at it by the poignant question asked of students in the very first session: "Do you feel pressed for time?"

I think it is fair to say that, in almost all of our schools today, the hands of most of our students would go up quickly in the affirmative. One of the concerns I hear most often, in my visits to schools throughout the country, has to do with the tight, highly structured schedule that most students—of all ages—live with, a schedule that is bound to rob them of some sense of imagination, spontaneity, and the sheer opportunity to enjoy life. That is the story of our time—it is something we frantically seek to manage as it presses upon us.

At first, the events of Holy Week, into which we now find ourselves, may seem a long way away from the "pressed for time" lives of our students (and, dare we add, their teachers and parents?). But these days are not meant just to be seen as memories that evoke "back when," a time long ago. They are meant in some way to be re-lived. That is what the Greek word, anamnesis, is all about: we do not simply recall something, we experience it all over again. God's time suddenly leaps over the centuries and presents itself to us anew. Just as we can re-live experiences we have had in the past with the same emotional intensity we encountered in the original event, Holy Week is about re-living Jesus' last days. All of a sudden they become new to us.

Time turns out to be something we are not simply pressed for, but something that impresses upon us. We have a rare opportunity this week: to enter into God's time.

The "Where" of Resurrection

April 10, 2012

Of the many questions raised by the biblical passages that describe Jesus' resurrection, an inevitable and common one has to do with the question of "where." Where is Jesus? Have they taken him away? Is he here or not? Where do we go now? There is an important reason for this, I believe. As much as Easter poses the question of "what?" (i.e., what actually happened with Jesus?), or, "who?," (i.e., who is this Jesus who has risen?), the "where?" is an essential part of the wondering and the proclaiming of what all of this means. It is not only an essential question about Jesus' whereabouts, but the question of where, in the here and now, do we find the message of Easter in our lives and in our communities?

Already, we are seeing signs of new life at Episcopal School of Jacksonville, following the tragedy a month ago. Longtime head of school there, Charles Zimmer, has graciously agreed to step in and serve as interim head, providing a sense of stability and longtime connection so needed at a critical time in the life of this community. A memorial fund has been established to honor Dale Regan. (You can read about it on their website, www.esj.org.) These are signs not only that life goes on, but that new life emerges out of pain and tragedy. They are the very practical examples and aftermaths of the basic Easter message of life triumphing over death. That is by no means to say that all of the shock and grief has passed—as with Jesus' risen body the wounds are still there. They have simply, and wonderfully, been redeemed.

In her Easter message, the Presiding Bishop has asked us to identify ways in which there is resurrected life in our parishes. We would do well to do the same in our school communities. Along with the questions of "What happened at Easter?" or, "What do we mean when we say there is life after death?" (all questions that many of our students will no doubt be asking), we can also be asking ourselves, collectively, the question that points to the very practical and tangible ways the Easter message is bearing fruit in our schools. Where is new life being found?

God's Inclusiveness

April 16, 2012

Two weeks ago I had the privilege of speaking with the board of trustees of Canterbury School in Greensboro, North Carolina, on the subject of Episcopal identity. There I was fortunate enough to see once again the Reverend Russell Ingersoll, former head of Christ School in Arden, North Carolina, and now a member of the Canterbury board. Over the years I have regarded Russ as one of the real pillars of Episcopal schools, embodying so much of what they stand for and can be.

During the meeting I was reminded of why I regard him as such a model. As we discussed a board's awareness of the Episcopal dimension of the school's mission, Russ made a remarkable comment. "God's inclusiveness is larger than our own inclusiveness," he observed.

On one level, I thought about the fact that, "At what other type of board meeting would one be gifted with such an observation?" Beyond that, however, Russ' comment was one of those worth not only pondering, but returning to, again and again.

For many people in our culture, the opposite of what he said is assumed. God represents less inclusivity than what we humans can possess. God represents the narrow way, the exclusionary way, the way of religion, as opposed to the openness of spirituality or a secular world-view. We enlightened human beings are supposedly moving beyond the narrowness of the God of religion. However the reverse is actually the case. Throughout the pages of the Bible, God is pushing people to more inclusivity, not less. God is the one, for example, who declares Cyrus, King of Persia, to be God's instrument for the liberation from exile. It is also Jesus who breaks beyond the restrictiveness of social or religious norms at the time and ministers to so many at the margins, bringing the whole world to himself.

We human beings may well have made some progress in our understanding of inclusivity, but it is God who challenges us to ever widening circles of care and openness to difference. We still have much to learn about our own limitations when it comes to accepting other peoples and groups. Fortunately, not only is God there to teach us what we have yet to learn, it is the very nature of God is to be inclusive.

That means that Episcopal schools are in an enviable position when it comes to being more inclusive, given the fact that we can talk about God and can spend time discerning what God is wanting from us. We possess a deep theological reason for wanting to be more inclusive.

A true reversal of what we might have thought to be the case! Imagine that, and it all stemmed from a school board meeting!

Calling All Introverts!

April 24, 2012

In case you have not yet noticed, there is a lot of writing going on these days about introverts. Lately, however, the tone of the writing is very different: it is not about introverts being "a problem," but about the actual advantages of introversion, even in the midst of what is a highly extroverted culture. As one writer describes them,

> Introverts....are oriented toward the inner life of thought; they tend to be reserved and cautious. They find social interactions draining, and they need solitude to recharge. It's not that introverts are antisocial as much as they appreciate fewer, more intimate friendships. They don't like small talk but appreciate deeper discussions.*

Of late I have been reading Susan Cain's book on the subject, *Quiet: The Power of Introverts in a World That Can't Stop Talking.* She has some very interesting things to say about how introverts can actually be effective leaders (I recall one search consultant saying that some of the best school heads are introverts that have learned how to do extroverted things), as well as talks of how the culture embodies extroversion to such a degree that it can make natural introverts (like me!) wince and retreat!

One of the things she alludes to but does not explicate in greater depth is the way in which our educational system is developing in such a way that it is not hospitable to introverts. To be sure, all introverts need to learn how to contribute to a classroom discussion, work in teams, and deal with the extroverts in their lives. But as we think about students we worry about—i.e., those who are not participating in class, or seem shy or withdrawn at times—are we judging them by extroverted standards?

An optimal learning experience is one in which both introverts and extroverts (and everyone in between!) can both feel at home as well as be able to work with those who project themselves differently. But is our teaching and learning tilted more toward extroversion than introversion? One of the ways that I have always attempted to make room for introverts in the conversation is—whether in leading a classroom discussion or working with a group of people—to ask a question and let the question linger, should no one immediately spring to answer it. There is uncomfortable silence for some, but not for all. In fact, it can be a small way to make room for the introvert—a group of people for whom the opportunity for reflection is so often welcome, not to mention uncommon!

*William Pannapacker, "Screening Out the Introverts," *The Chronicle of Higher Education* (April 20, 2012), A27.

Springtime Challenges

April 30, 2012

This time of year usually finds most of us making some type of transition in the clothes we wear. Out comes the spring wardrobe, although in many parts of the country, that transition might have taken place much earlier than usual, given that the first three months of 2012 were the warmest first three months of the year on record!

There is a certain type of "seasonal wear" that schools take on, this time of year. It is what, in the words of the authors of one of my favorite books, is called, "The armor of busyness."* We equip ourselves, defend ourselves, by being ultra busy. Consequently, the days following spring vacation and leading up to the end of school feel more like a mad dash than a culmination, and can leave us breathless and fatigued, wondering where the days and weeks went.

Like all armor, this armor of busyness wards off things. In some cases, it wards off the needs of others. Being so over-scheduled, racing against time, we may well be less attentive to what is going on around us. The needs of people—which can be great this time of year—get overlooked or silenced, all in the service of getting it all done.

As mayor of Newark, New Jersey, Cory Booker is no doubt a

busy man. All seasons are times of busyness and overload for him. Recently Booker was returning home and discovered that his next-door neighbor's house was on fire. Even though his security detail tried to detain him, Booker ran into the building having heard the faint calls of, "Help! I'm here!" They were coming from the bedroom, where his neighbor was trapped. Booker found her, retrieved her, and carried her on his shoulders, through the burning kitchen, to the outside. Shunning any claim to heroism, Booker claimed that he did what he did on instinct, fighting against tremendous fear for his own life. "I didn't feel bravery, I felt terror," he reported. Booker came to refer to this event as his, "Come to Jesus moment," a time when, having shed the armor of busyness, he was once again reminded of what is truly important in life.

Our challenge, this spring, is not to be too busy to miss the faint cries of, "Help! I'm here!" They may dislodge us from all that we must do, but they also hold the potential of bringing out the best in us.

*As quoted in Laurent A. Parks Daloz, Cheryl H. Keen, James P. Keen, and Sharon Parks Daloz, *Common Fire: Leading Lives of Commitment in a Complex World* (Boston: Beacon Press, 1996), 11.

Springtime Challenges II

May 7, 2012

The April 22nd edition of the *New York Times* carried a very sobering article about our highly-connected world. Writing on the topic, "The Flight from Conversation," M.I.T. psychologist Sherry Turkle addressed the irony of how, in a culture where we are always communicating and constantly are connected, we are actually spending more time hiding from each other, being alone together, and keeping each other at bay. The big casualty, in her view, is the activity of conversation, where we truly tend to one another and see things from another person's perspective. Today, in her words, "We expect more from technology and less from one another," with no time for the patience, self-reflection, and slower pace that real conversation requires. This means that not only have our hand-held devices altered what we do, but actually who we are.

Turkle's remedies include the introduction of "device-free zones," be it at home, work, or school (something she ironically calls, "sacred space"). The other suggestion she offers is that we adults intentionally model real conversation to our children.

As I thought about her suggestions, particularly that latter one, I thought, "Have we come to this, that we actually need to model real conversation to our children or our students?" While I do not agree with the fullness of Turkle's rather dismal diagnosis, I think there is real merit in the activity of modeling conversation. At some level, I think we collectively understand what is at stake, for as much as conversation is up for grabs in our highly-connected world, the national discourse at so many levels contains more references to the notion of having conversations on difficult issues as at any time in the past. We can tell what is missing by the many references to its importance as a solution.

Springtime in the life of a school is a period where any number of important conversations need to take place, but often do not for sheer lack of time. As we begin to bring closure to a busy school year, what things need to be both said and heard—reflecting the two-way nature of conversation—that have not yet taken place, be it between two people or within our school community? What conversations need to occur that will help bring the year to an appropriate conclusion, as opposed to leaving things dangling in the rush to the finish?

No matter how connected we are, there is no substitute for real conversation. Perhaps we do need as adults to model this more intentionally for the sake of our students, particularly during the time of year when—as difficult as it can be—it is most needed.

Setting Limits

May 14, 2012

This past weekend brought the tragic news of the death of the Reverend Mary-Marguerite Kohn, co-rector of St. Peter's Episcopal Church in Ellicott City, Maryland. Ms. Kohn died of wounds sustained on May 3rd, when she was shot by a homeless person while working in the church. Brenda Brewington, an employee at the parish and formerly on the staff of the preschool at St. Peter's, was also shot by the same person and died that very day.

Apparently Ms. Kohn had informed a homeless person that he had to limit the number of visits he was making to the parish's food pantry. When he heard this news he allegedly became belligerent and subsequently returned to the church with a gun.

As with the March tragedy in Jacksonville, the response of parishioners and the diocese has been extraordinary. Likewise, the quick response of nearby St. John's Church in Ellicott City, opening its doors to St. Peter's parishioners immediately after the tragedy, was inspiring.

For the second time in two months, dedicated leaders of an Episcopal parish or school community have died in the service of their work. Like Dale Regan at Episcopal School of Jacksonville, Ms. Kohn had made a decision to set some limits, in this case in line with the policy of the food pantry. As in Jacksonville, the decision to do this prompted a violent reaction, ending in the deaths of both victims and assailants.

We are left with so many perplexing questions, following upon these two tragedies. We may ask, "What has happened to a society where the mere setting of limits prompts such violent responses?" Likewise, "How have we progressed to the point where unstable people have such easy access to firearms?" These and other perplexing questions may well lead us to the even greater question, "Has it come to this?"

Lurking in the heart of those who lead may well be another question, "Is this a dangerous business, setting limits?" "How risky is it, today, to make difficult decisions?" From the news we have received over the past two months, the answer may seem clear: it is pretty risky. What's more, as I thought over the reactions I had to both tragedies, I also thought about those potential leaders of our churches and school, who see such events taking place and may end up wondering, "Is this really the kind of work I want to be doing?"

Those are all understandable concerns and conclusions. In far less tragic ways, we have all come to realize that it is much tougher to set limits today in a culture of entitlement. But that does not mean that those limits are any less important, any less needed. Truly, leadership today demands an ongoing defining of boundaries, helping people to understand that there are consequences to actions, even when it can feel unsafe doing so. Sadly, far too few people are doing this type of important work in our culture. This task of setting limits has always been a courageous part of the work of every leader. These two tragedies have reminded us that it takes more courage than ever.

The Privilege of Service

May 21, 2012

I had the great honor of preaching this month at the farewell Eucharist for Lucy Nazro, who retires this June after thirty-two years as head of school at St. Andrew's Episcopal School in Austin Texas. As you may well know, Lucy is an icon of Episcopal school leadership, a symbol of what it means to build up a school proud of and seeking to live out its Episcopal identity. The extent and variety of the turnout for the service was alone a great tribute to her leadership. Likewise, there were many wonderful and deeply felt things said about her. As Lucy remarked, after the service, in her characteristic, self-effacing humor, "Who is this person they were all talking about?"

At the end of the offertory presentations done in her honor, Bishop Harrison asked if Lucy had anything to say. Lucy's response was simple, but powerful: "What a privilege it is in life to find oneself wholeheartedly dedicated to something."

This is the time of year when schools honor those people who have indeed given their lives in service to the school community. Whether they are the leaders of the school, longtime members of the faculty, or people on the staff who have served as the thread that in some way holds a school community together, they are the type of people who make us wonder, "What will this school be like without them?" As we honor them, we honor the reality that schools are, above all, about people, who go about their daily work with a sense of mission and purpose that serves to build up the life of the school and pave the way as an example to others. So, too, like Lucy, they remind us not only of the impact that many years of service can have, but also the deep sense of blessing and satisfaction that results from giving oneself wholeheartedly to a place. They not only define the life of a school, but their commitment to the school has defined their lives. No greater satisfaction can be had than the experience of those two types of definitions meeting.

In Jesus' words, "Well done, good and faithful servants." These people have given what, as Wordsworth once put it, "that best portion of a good person's life." In the end, it all comes to thanks: the thanks we feel for the impact they have had, the thanks that these fine people feel for the rare opportunity they have had.

Shedding Light

June 4, 2012

You may have heard the story of Trish Vickers, a resident of Lyme Regis in Great Britain. Having lost her sight, she decided to devote her life to the writing of a novel in longhand. Each day she would take pen in hand and attempt to make slow but steady progress in her writing. After one particularly long and intense session, where Vickers had written twenty-six pages of narrative, she learned something devastating: the pen she had been using for these many pages had been dry and all the pages were blank.

Vickers turned to the fingerprinting department of the Lyme Regis police for help. Using special lighting techniques, they were able to recover the writing from the impressions on the pages. Forensic specialist Kerry Savage was able to bring the writing to light, spending her lunch hours doing the work day after day. As Savage observed, "It was nice to be able to do something for somebody."

Schools are very busy places where a lot is accomplished, each day. Our obvious business is about learning, exploring, growing into a community, getting through the schedule, and getting things done. Less obvious is what goes on underneath all of the business as usual, something akin to what the fingerprinting department did for Trish Vickers: the small acts of generosity, problem solving, helping people to see things from a different perspective. In short, it is about the shedding of light, helping our students and our colleagues to see events and experiences another way. A teacher guides a student toward understanding that the problem he or she is encountering offers hope, not just discouragement. "Have you ever thought of it this way?" an advisor asks an advisee, helping that student to view the task of making a decision through a new lens. "This is difficult stuff," a teacher explains to her class as they tackle a complex subject, thereby both comforting them and challenging them. "This was a very tough loss, but our true test is in how we bounce back," a coach tells his players following a last-minute defeat, offering hope at a time of deep disappointment. In these and countless other acts of care, we offer another solution to a dilemma, a new way of looking at something, the re-interpretation of an experience that initially seemed to be a dead end. Thanks to our hard work, things are no longer the way they initially seemed.

We shed a lot of light in our daily work, and in so doing we make school more than about just getting things done. We make it a true place of light.

2012-2013

Returning to School!

August 20, 2012

As we resume our Weekly Meditation series, I would like to welcome all of you back for the new academic year. Some of you are already in session; others are getting ready with purpose and intensity; still others are savoring that last bit of summer before things begin to get really busy. Whatever situation this message finds you experiencing, I wish you a very good beginning, and thank you for all of your support of NAES.

In Liz Moore's new novel, *Heft*, Kel Keller is a high school student who comes from a very troubled family situation. One night his mother attempts to take her own life, and Kel both calls 911 and spends time with her at the hospital. He departs from the hospital after a very long evening, with his mother's condition stable, and begins to drive.

At first he does not know where to go; he just drives. Then he ends up in the parking lot of his school. It is the middle of the night. "It is a comfort to me to see the building," he tells the reader. "At school I am generally happy and relaxed. At school I have friends and am respected." He sits there a long time.

All across the country, students are returning to Episcopal schools, in many cases they show their faces well ahead of the first day of classes. For so many of them, this school means a great deal. It is here that they find nourishment, happiness, friends, community, and respect. For a great many of them, this is the place that is at the center of their lives, and it is to this place that they return both in happy moments as well as in moments of crisis and disappointment.

As we return to our schools and notice just how important this place is to so many students, I hope you find yourself catching their enthusiasm. We may feel some ambivalence about getting back into the routine, yet the esteem in which our students hold their school will surely carry us a long way into the new academic year.

In Praise of Awe

August 27, 2012

In a recent article that appeared on LiveScience.com, Melanie Rudd came to some interesting conclusions about the role of awe in our lives. As she put it, gazing at a mountain vista, a stunning landscape, or listening to a great symphony may well turn out to help people feel less rushed, more patient, and more compassionate toward others. "Stanford University researchers have discovered that awe—as opposed to joy or other positive emotions—gives people the sense that time has slowed down."*

Rudd showed one group of volunteers a video of such awe-inspiring scenes as the ones mentioned above. Another group saw a video of a confetti-laden parade. The impact was telling: the first group that saw the scenes capable of producing awe reported feeling less hurried. What's more, they turned out to be, as a group, more likely to donate their money to charity, less absorbed with materials goods, and generally reported higher levels of satisfaction with their lives.

There are few things that we hope more for our students than that they feel less rushed in the rat race of life, more patient, and more compassionate toward others. So, too, we wish them to be generous, less materialistic, and feel a certain level of satisfaction with life. In these and other goals we share common ground and hold to common hopes for our students as do those in non-sectarian schools.

What we uniquely possess, in Episcopal schools, is the possibility of allowing opportunities, on a regular basis, for moments of awe. School chapel provides us with an inbuilt opportunity both to make reference to the experience of awe and to invite students to experience it within the context of worship. From what the research above indicates, it may turn out that such moments are less a diversion from the regular routine of school life than a profound influence on that routine. With less rushed, more patient, and more compassionate students in our schools, the bonds of our community life may be strengthened and the quality of that life deeply improved. Awe might well be the key to the school culture we seek to develop this school year, something well within the reach of every Episcopal school!

*See, Melanie Rudd, "Awe to nourish the soul," *This Week* (August 10, 2012), 19.

The Hidden Dimensions
of Episcopal Identity

September 4, 2012

It is not uncommon to hear, from many of our schools, of the experience of hiring marketing firms to find out what attracts families to those schools. When the results are shared, and the top reasons for why families are drawn to or stay at the school are listed, there is frequent surprise that there is much less reference to "being Episcopal" than might have initially been imagined.

Of course, it is easy to forget that an increasingly smaller percentage of the general population these days—including many in our very schools—is actually familiar with the word, "Episcopal," at all. But, as Peter Barrett, head of school at St. Patrick's Episcopal Day School in Washington, DC pointed out a few years ago, if the word, "Episcopal," does not appear in the proverbial "top ten," then take a closer look at the other things that do appear on that list. Chances are that many of them relate quite significantly to a school's understanding of itself as an Episcopal school.

Colson Whitehead is a very promising and talented young writer. He is also a graduate of an Episcopal school. To be sure, he has often written about some of the "cultural excess" that can be found among those who attend privileged independent schools, and what it is like to feel at the margins of that type of culture. To the best of my knowledge, he has not addressed the matter of going specifically to an Episcopal school, and what that might have meant to him.

In the July 29, 2012 edition of the *New York Times Book Review*, Mr. Whitehead wrote a very insightful piece on the subject, "How to Write," and while the word, "Episcopal," never appears in the short article, I had the clear sense that the values of an Episcopal school clearly came through in the advice he had for young, aspiring writers. Among those pieces of advice he gave:

- Don't go searching for a subject, let your subject find you. You can't rush inspiration.
- Listen to your heart. "Ask your heart, Is it true? And if it is, let it be."
- "What isn't said is as important as what is said."
- Make use of writer's block: "The gods of creativity bless you, they forsake you, it's out of your hands and whatnot."
- "Revise. Revise. Revise."

I may well be reading more than I should be into what he says, but I see the influence of an Episcopal school, with its emphasis on grace, the unspoken as well as the spoken, and the redemptive value of setbacks and diligence, all through his words.

Among these trees of wisdom, I sense the presence of an Episcopal school forest!

Back-to-School Nights and Days

September 10, 2012

I recall a back-to-school evening at the school I was working at, some years ago, where I had just finished completing a summary of the course I was teaching to these parents' children. It was a quick summary, given the brevity of time I had with them. When I asked the group if they had any questions about the course there was silence. Then a father modestly remarked, "I'm still getting over having to climb all of those steps to get up here to this classroom!"

All of us know the characteristic remarks we hear from parents on such evenings (perhaps, "I wish I could be taking this course" is one of the most common). But there are also frequent remarks about the sheer intensity of their children's schedules, how much is packed into one day, indeed how going through an abbreviated schedule of their children's regular day alone can be an ordeal for so many of them.

These remarks remind us of the sheer intensity of school life. We are also reminded of it at the very beginning of the school year, when our colleagues on the faculty remark about how, over the summer, they had gotten used to a much more leisurely pace to life. Now the body and spirit are being required to step up the tempo with the advent of another school year, and it is not an easy transition to make.

Our schools are blessed with a rich array of offerings, making for a tightly-packed yet abundant day for every student. We often forget, however, just how intense these days can be, individually or strung together. As I have worked with many school chaplains, over the years, who have had difficulty making the adjustment from parish work to school work, the intensity and rapid pace of school life is among the top reasons why some chaplains find that transition to be a difficult one. We cannot underestimate what a challenge this can be for both young and old.

I, of course, share the concerns I have heard throughout our country, from our member schools, about the lack of down time in the lives of young people, or the cost of overscheduling our students. Does this put their imaginations, creativity, playfulness, and spontaneity at risk? We may not be able to answer these questions at the moment, nor be able to stem the larger cultural tide and the pressures it puts on children and young people. But if we are to be serious about looking at our school cultures, we have to be thinking about the intensity of school life. Moreover, if we are to take seriously the biblical distinction between God's time and our own time, then we cannot avoid an intentional examination of the pace we create for our students and faculty.

Loving What Is Mortal

September 17, 2012

This past Monday, September 10th, was the poet, Mary Oliver's, 77th birthday. She happens to be among my favorite poets, as I suspect she is for many of you. I regard her continual example of waiting upon life to reveal its graces to us as something I need to be reminded of on quite a regular basis!

In her poem, "In Backwater Woods," Mary Oliver speaks of how, in the end, there are but three things we must be able to do in life. The first is both simple and challenging: as she puts it, "To love what is mortal."

One of the wonderful things about Episcopal schools is their continual drive to be better. Over and over again I have seen schools look seriously at what needs to be improved in their common life and have made sincere—and often successful—attempts to improve that common life. We are seekers after truth, and part of the drive to improve is to draw nearer to that truth. It is that drive toward excellence, toward truth, that shapes us and, in so many cases, defines who we are as educators and as places that dare to be idealistic in the world today.

At the same time, we are, on a regular basis, reminded of, indeed thrown back upon, our humanity. We are mortal beings that, together, comprise a mortal institution. That is at one and the same time both painfully obvious but something we are eager to forget. As much as we seek to improve upon our abilities and performance, we also face the challenge of accepting our limitations. That is as difficult a challenge as any steps we might take toward improvement.

Mary Oliver challenges us to hold that mortality dear to our hearts. That need not hold us back, for it is Immortal Love that equips us to love what is mortal, and that same Immortal Love also is calling and equipping us to be better people, better communities.

I think I have pretty solid grounds in saying that most of our school communities, at some point in this coming year, will have to come face to face with just how utterly human we actually are. Can we embrace that humanity, when it comes reminding us of its lingering presence? Can we hold dear what is mortal about our schools?

Changing Our Minds and Hearts

September 24, 2012

There is a famous story told about Mahatma Gandhi. Once he was accused by an angry opponent of having no integrity, as what he said one week was contrary to what he had said the previous week. Gandhi, unperturbed by this accusation, told his opponent that he was correct about the discrepancy, but said it was due to the fact that, "I have learned something since last week."

A poignant example, to be sure, of what we educators so believe: learning has the power to change people. We may go from asking a question to finding an answer, or being one week certain of the answer and finding ourselves the next week asking questions about that answer. As the world opens up to us, through education, and we come face to face with ideas we had never encountered or considered, we can experience the deep blessing of transformation. I dare say that one of the reasons most of us have committed ourselves to being in Episcopal schools is that we have undergone such an experience of transformation through our own years of formal education. We know what new worlds are to be found through that process, and we yearn to provide the opportunity to help our students experience just that.

Increasingly I am concerned about how that message of change, be it in our minds or hearts (or both!), is verboten in our culture. Polls are telling us that the electorate in our country has already made up its mind in a way never seen before; to be "undecided" is to be in a tiny minority, and positions have hardened to such a degree that change is seen as a weakness. Likewise, we seem more to use the wonders of technology to reinforce our existing beliefs than expand or adjust them, let alone respectfully hear what the other side may have to say. Sociologist Tim Clydesdale tells us that college students are showing increasing tendencies to put their convictions and values in a "lockbox" as they head off to college, leaving them immune to change as opposed to allowing time to reflect on who they are and what they believe.

Few things are more important in our respective mission statements than our hope to produce young people who have conviction, who are willing to take a stand, and who feel passionate about how they view the world. But do we allow for the opportunity to change, to feel differently about something as a result of an idea just encountered, a perspective never before considered, as was the case with Gandhi? For a culture increasingly polarized and fixed upon a rush to judgment about the opposing view, a change of mind and heart may be increasingly unwelcome. To that culture we have a message that needs to be loud and clear: Episcopal schools hold out the potential that people can indeed change as a result of their education.

Cheating: Bad News and Good News

October 1, 2012

Even at this early stage of the academic year, we are reminded of just how perennial the issue of cheating can be. This month, Stuyvesant High School in New York City (a highly competitive public high school) suspended 12 students and threatened to suspend 50 more, claiming that these students allegedly shared test answers via text and email. Harvard University has accused 125 undergraduates of allegedly sharing and plagiarizing answers for a final take-home exam in, of all ironies, an "Introduction to Congress" course. Our discouragement upon hearing such news is often accompanied by the sobering realization that such things could easily happen in our own school.

The news about cheating may be disheartening. However, there is also some good news, and the type of news that dovetails quite nicely with the very mission and culture of Episcopal schools.

In a *Wall Street Journal* article last May,* Duke University scientist, Dan Ariely, raised the question of what prompts people to be honest. His findings were both dramatic and encouraging, given who and what we are as Episcopal schools. Ariely worked with different control groups who were given a very easy opportunity to cheat on a project. Among those who, prior to the opportunity, were asked to recite the Ten Commandments or other classic moral codes, the rate of cheating was much lower than that of those groups who had no such moral reminders. He even found this to be the case in one control group made up entirely of agnostics or atheists. He concluded that the simple and routine reminding of people of moral codes has a significant influence on behavior. As he put it, "While ethics lectures and training seem to have little to no effect on people, reminders of morality have an outsize effect on behavior."

Given our responsibility, in Episcopal schools, to be reminding our students and staff of the rich moral tradition from which our schools have developed, not to mention the opportunities etched into our daily schedule to provide such reminders (i.e., chapel), it just may be that we have a tremendous opportunity to instill in students some of the most persuasive and effective reasons to uphold and promote honesty. It may well be that the seed of an answer to one of our schools' most persistent moral challenges can be found right in our respective backyards!

*See, Dan Ariely, "Why We Lie," *The Wall Street Journal* (May 26, 2012).

The Humming Chorus

October 8, 2012

I confess to being quite an opera fan. (It is my one great New York City indulgence!) One of my favorite sections of any opera occurs in Puccini's *Madama Butterfly*. Cio-Cio San (Madama Butterfly), a young Japanese woman, has been waiting for her husband, the American Lt. Pinkerton, to return to her after a number of years. Once she has spotted his ship in the harbor, she sits patiently with her young son for his return. As the chorus offstage hums a haunting, wordless, and altogether disarming melody, we watch as Cio-Cio San does nothing but wait.

Nothing but wait!

It is a heartbreaking moment in opera, as we sense that her wait may well be in vain. As those closest to her warn, Lt. Pinkerton may never return to her. Still, she sits there in hope, and there is true dignity in her demeanor and sheer simplicity of purpose.

The Humming Chorus has turned out to be an increasing help to me this past year. As I stand in line to wait (something that is very much a part of life in New York City), find myself on hold on the telephone, or find the seconds it takes for my computer to move along feeling more like hours, I have been humming the chorus from that opera. It helps remind me that there is hope, purpose, and openness to be found in waiting, just like we witness on stage with Cio-Cio San.

We are experiencing an interesting cross-current in modern life. On the one hand, the speed with which we live our lives is ever increasing, and that is making the time we spend waiting increasingly hard to endure. We stand in line or suffer through the time on hold to thinking that this is not the way life should be. We do not deserve this. We should be moving on to other, more important things.

For me, it may be the Humming Chorus. For others, it may be a prayer to God. Still, for others, it might be the opportunity to start a conversation with a fellow waiter-in-line. Whatever it may be, we need some help not only in making the waiting time tolerable but in retrieving the belief that there is true dignity in waiting. As the Psalmist writes, "My soul waits for the LORD, more than watchmen for the morning, more than watchmen for the morning" (Ps. 130:5). Contrary to the implicit messages we get from a culture of speed, we are not diminished as human beings in our waiting time.

Identity and Identities

October 15, 2012

An article in the September 3rd edition of the *New York Times* revealed a trend which, no doubt, is surprising to many.* Increasing numbers of international Muslim students are drawn to Roman Catholic colleges and universities in the United States. Over the past decade, the population of Muslim students from overseas attending Catholic institutions has nearly doubled, while the population of Muslim women from abroad attending such colleges during this time has nearly tripled. This may be all the more surprising since there has been no intentional recruiting campaign for these students. As one administrator at a Catholic university explained, "It is basically something that happened through word of mouth and reputation."

Even more surprising may be the reasons these students give for attending Catholic institutions. As one student observed, "On the whole, I like the fact that there is faith, even if it is not my faith, and I feel that my faith is respected."

This is not to say that the transition is an easy one, or that there are not initial intimidations. In the long haul, however, these Muslim students indicated a preference for a place where religious belief and practice is honored, where there were compelling reasons for service to the community, and where religious questions could be pursued in the classroom. These factors allow not only Catholics to practice their faith, but seem to encourage a general openness to and allowance for all religious traditions to flourish. In the words of one Muslim student, "I don't have to leave my faith at home when I come to school."

Once again, we see a poignant example of what many in Episcopal schools have learned: adherence to a particular faith tradition is not a deterrent to religious diversity, it can in fact serve as a catalyst for it. It turns out to be a welcoming mat. To many secularists, this may be hard to understand. How can a school with a clear and particular faith tradition be in any way appealing to an alternative tradition? I think it has to do with what may well be an overused word these days: authenticity. When we are authentically ourselves, others different from us are invited to do the same. Our differences are not smoothed over or ignored; rather, we come to a common table with a confidence that we have both something to give and something to learn. The results, as the article indicates, can be surprising.

*See, Richard Pérez-Peña, "Muslims from Abroad are Thriving in Catholic Colleges," *The New York Times* (September 3, 2012), A12.

The Two-Eyed Life

October 22, 2012

Recently I had the privilege of receiving a copy of a new book, published by St. Andrew's Episcopal School in Austin, Texas. Entitled, *Faithfully, Lucy*, it is a collection of Lucy Nazro's chapel sermons, as well as her talks on different occasions in the life of that school. As many of you know, Lucy retired last summer after serving 30 years as head of school at St. Andrew's. It is a fitting tribute to a person who, as head of school, not only did chapel on a regular basis, but took her role as the spiritual leader of the school very seriously.

Faithfully, Lucy, is a treasure trove of spiritual and deeply pastoral reflections on the life of a school, be it at the end of a difficult but redemptive football season or at the loss of a member of the school community. Lucy's words betray an understanding of the power and rhythm of school life. Most of all, I was struck by Lucy's considerable theological insights, particularly as she spots subtle but instructive aspects of biblical passages that speak to the issues she was addressing.

I was particularly taken by some thoughts she shared on a parent evening about being an Episcopal school. Drawing upon Parker Palmer's notion that we often live "one-eyed lives," Lucy said this:

With the mind's eye we see a world of fact and reason. It is a cold and mechanical place, but we have built our lives there because it seemed predictable and safe…. [But] we open the eye of the heart and we see another sight: a world warmed and transformed by the power of love, a vision of community beyond the mind's capacity to see. We cannot forsake our hearts, and yet we cannot abandon our minds. How shall we use both eyes not to create a blurry double image, but one world, in all its dimensions, healed and made whole?

In Episcopal schools, we definitely need to teach our students to use both eyes…. This ability cannot be taught in one or two lessons. I believe it is taught only through years of experiencing it: in chapel, in hearing God's word, in singing the hymns of the Church, in prayer, in silence, and in community service, in meeting heart to heart with people who need us— the aged, the hungry, the lonely, the homeless.

The most wonderful thing about this and other passages in the book is that I can, so clearly, hear Lucy saying these things, knowing how reflective they are of the core of her being. Truly, in our schools we teach the two-eyed life through those teachers and leaders whose words are made all the more credible to students and their families by the power of their example.

Sure Indicators

October 29, 2012

Last week I had the great pleasure of visiting the Episcopal School of Los Angeles, one of two new Episcopal schools to open this autumn (the other being Trinity Episcopal Day School in Hartford, Connecticut). Episcopal School of Los Angeles opened its doors to twenty-eight students in grades six, seven, and eight, at its facility in the heart of Hollywood. As you can imagine, it was a tremendously exciting experience to see a school in its very early stages, brimming with life and hope, the culmination of years of intense and courageous planning.

The opening of any new school is, of course, a great experiment, and there are many challenges that the school faces, as one would expect. Facilities, funding, and establishing a niche in a competitive independent school market remain among the most obvious and pressing challenges. Still, confidence and determination abound in this new school: as with so many of our new schools, there is strong and widespread belief in its mission and—correspondingly—a strong reservoir of support for it.

Although there are many obstacles and uncertainties looming ahead for the school, I experienced a moment at lunchtime when I felt certain that this school—as with many like it—was going to make it. As we were finishing our meal, I looked around at the neighboring tables. There I saw students who had finished their lunch and were talking comfortably and excitedly with their teachers, enjoying what on the surface seemed to be a nice pause in the day. But such moments are not simply diversions, they are at the core of what we try to create and nourish in the culture of our schools. As I saw students interacting with their teachers, I sensed that a crucial goal had already been achieved, a goal that is at the core of the school's mission.

Simple, but essential, interaction between teachers and students: to me, it was as clear an indication as could be found that this school was not only on its way toward flourishing, but was truly flourishing already. What's more, it remains one of the key elements to the flourishing of all of our schools.

Two Worlds

November 5, 2012

Returning to New York City a few days after Sandy hit was, as you can imagine, quite a strange experience for me. A sense of sobriety hangs over the city, long lines of people wrap around street corners as residents seek to get to places where the subway cannot, at the moment, take them, and incredible acts of graciousness and patience intermingle with clear signs that New Yorkers have had their fill of post-Sandy hardships.

Nothing is stranger, however, than the dividing line between those who live and work north of 40th Street and those who live and work south of it. Those who have power belong to the first group; the second group lives without power. Two worlds—as some TV journalists have referred to it, in their post-Sandy coverage, as, "a tale of two cities"—and I currently happen to work in one world (where there is power) and live in the other (the one without power).

The difference in these worlds is striking. Life above 40th Street seems normal, bustling and seemingly undaunted by Sandy's rage. Cross 40th Street and one enters a different realm: there are no traffic lights or pedestrian signs at crosswalks, traffic is much lighter (who would want to drive in a part of Manhattan without traffic signals?), and there is a much more tentative sense about things. Things seem eerily quiet. One gets a clear sense that something has happened here. As darkness descends, the gap between the two worlds is all the more dramatic.

As I crossed over from one world to the next, I thought about the students who attend our schools across the country that travel from one world to the next each day of their lives, or the faculty or staff member who makes a daily transition from one neighborhood to another, thereby entering into a very different cultural and economic environment each time they come to work.

Those transitions may not be as immediate or dramatic as the one currently to be experienced between north and south of 40th Street in New York City, but the daily movement between their own two worlds is something that both challenges them and shapes them as they go about being a part of our school communities.

Who are the people in your school community that make this shift between two worlds each day? What is it like for them to engage in this pattern of life and work? Is this something they get used to, or do they experience a daily reminder of just what a distance they travel regularly—a distance not necessarily measured by miles but by ethos? Moreover, what blessings do they bestow upon your school by virtue of the transition they make each day? How is your school made better by their presence, by the distance they have traveled?

Chaplain or Chaplin?

November 12, 2012

Of the many surprises I experienced during my years as a school or college chaplain, one surely stands out: how is it possible that, in communities of highly intelligent people, so often the position I held was spelled, "Chaplin," instead of, "Chaplain?" I could not count the number of times I received messages that began, "Chaplin Heischman." Be it students or adults, it happened often and repeatedly enough that I ended up asking myself, "Is there some connection between what I am doing and Charlie Chaplin? Is there something I am missing here?"

Recently, as I was reading the reviews of the new Broadway show, *Chaplin*, I was reminded of those recurring misspellings of the position I once held. I ended up thinking about the possible parallels between the work of a chaplain in our schools and the work of one of film's most creative and significant artists.

Chaplin was trained in ballet, which allowed him to do amazing stunts and make use of his incredible physical agility. Without saying a word, Chaplin told such interesting stories with his body. A good chaplain, to my mind, needs to have at least a little bit of artistry inside of him or her, be it of the dramatic, musical, or improvisational variety. So, too, Chaplin was able, in his films, to communicate the simple reality that life can be hard, sometimes unfair, and he did that so often by focusing on those who were experiencing difficult times. One of the most important gifts a chaplain can give to a school is the understanding of these realities of life, particularly in environments steeped in a system of merits and rewards.

It is in Chaplin's use of silence, however, that I think we find the greatest connection between a "chaplain" and the "Chaplin." Silence, for Chaplin, provided an opportunity for storytelling; it was not a technical inhibition of film at that time or a disadvantage in his portrayal of characters. There were ways that silence could be used in his artistry that words could not capture.

Perhaps that is why, after a sustained period of time when chaplains have introduced school communities to the ways silence can be used in chapel, students and faculty alike begin to crave it. The chaplain in our schools can be the one who ushers us into the possibilities of silence, rather than seeing it simply as an absence of what normally is crammed into our days.

Whether it is an offering of prayers without words, or allowing a poignant moment to linger, the link between chaplain and Chaplin can be strong. Maybe I don't mind the misspelling that much, after all!

Because We Are...

November 19, 2012

In his latest book, *Sacred Ground*, Eboo Patel (our Biennial keynote speaker in 2010), tells the story of the time he was scheduled to speak at Berea College in Kentucky. It was planned that he speak in the college chapel, and prior to the event he was asked by college officials if he wanted the cross, which is prominently centered at the front of the chapel, to be removed. No doubt this question was asked out of a deep sensitivity, given that Patel is a devout Muslim.

Patel's response, however, may have surprised both college officials and a number of us who work in religiously diverse environments. As he considered the Christian roots of Berea College, he thought about the fact that it was the Christian foundation of the college that led to the moment when a Muslim speaker would be invited to speak not only on campus, but in the college chapel. Hence, Patel replied:

> I don't want them to cover the cross. I don't want them to hide their Christian faith. I want them to tell the story of how that cross inspired them to build an interracial college in pre-Civil War Kentucky. I want them to share how that cross moves them to admit Buddhists from Sri Lanka and Hindus

from India, and have them in classes and volunteer activities with Christians from Appalachia. I want them to tell the world, "This is what it means to be Christian."

Granted, Patel is a person comfortable in a variety of explicitly religious contexts, representative of a wide variety of traditions. Still, his words pose both a challenge to us as well as a different way of thinking about how we in Episcopal schools interface with a wide variety of religious traditions. Rather than implying that it is in spite of the fact that we are Christian or Episcopalian that we welcome a variety of religious traditions into our schools, it is because of our identity as such that we welcome others that are different from us.

Truly, how ironic it is that often it takes someone from a tradition other than our own to help us understand who we are and what we should be doing.

Words with Practices Attached

November 26, 2012

Among the many remarkable observations made by Krista Tippett, at our Biennial Conference, I most remember something she said almost in passing, but something which, I believe, gets to the heart of what teaching is all about.

In speaking about the importance of words in our efforts to promote more civil conversations, Tippett mentioned that teachers have a particularly important and symbolic role in this effort. Teachers, she told us, connect their words with practices and virtues. We are the people who speak words that have practices attached to them.

To be sure, teachers are true lovers of words. Whether it is the challenge words pose to us, or in the search to find the right use of words to express ourselves, words give teaching life. What we may be less aware of is the degree to which we seek to connect words with intention, respect, and context. We have the opportunity to help our students learn how to disagree with one another in a spirit of honor and compassion; we see in our empathy with the struggles of young people just how powerful and hurtful words can be; and we carry with us the duty to speak about our colleagues in a manner which promotes the overall good will and positive spirit of the school community.

When we combine our love of words with those practices that, as Tippett reminded us, build up the common life, then we are the truest models of what she refers to when she speaks of, "words that have practices attached to them." That modeling is not done in a vacuum, for we do this in the midst of a group of students—whatever age they may be—that are seeking models of the very connection between words and practices that Tippett mentioned in her keynote address.

Often we do that work in ways we do not recognize or understand, at first glance. What most strikes me, as I speak with groups of students at Episcopal schools throughout the country, is the answer they almost invariably give to the question, "Why do you like this school?" With amazing consistency, in almost every school, they reply quickly and enthusiastically, "Our teachers are always ready to be of help," "they spend so much extra time with us outside of class," "they show they really care." I think that is something of what Tippett spoke of: we not only tell students we are ready to be of help, we connect those words with the practice of being available.

Could there be any greater challenge than linking our words with practices? Could there be any greater tribute to what teaching is all about, and the influence we teachers assuredly can have, than helping young people to see the all-important way in which their lives can be graced with words and practices brought together? Challenging as it may be, we are doing a lot of that connecting already, in ways that our students recognize and point to with great pride.

Waking Up to Advent

December 3, 2012

The whole secret of the teacher's force lies in the conviction that humans are convertible. And they are. They want awakening.

– Ralph Waldo Emerson

I thought about these words of Ralph Waldo Emerson as we approached Advent. He speaks not only about the highest calling of teachers—to awaken students to the opportunities and widening visions of learning, but also to the innate yearning of students to be awakened. It is not a matter of imposing something on students against their will; rather, we are engaged in the process of awakening because that is what students seek from us at the deepest level.

Emerson added that this is not just the vocation of the teacher with a spiritual vision, for, in his view, all teachers—sectarian or secular—are committed to trying to, "get the soul out of bed, out of her deep habitual sleep."

This is also the task of Advent—to awaken ourselves to the promises that surround us that speak of Christ's coming; in other words, to get our souls out of bed. So, too, they speak to the irony of Advent awakening, of how in the midst of one of the busiest and most hectic seasons of the year—be it within school or without—we have this capacity, as human beings, to be habitually in deep spiritual slumber. It may be boredom and routine, an astonishingly high threshold for gaining our attention, or from having our faces continually buried in hand-held devices. Whatever it may be, we cry out for an awakening, even in the midst of times that seem most demanding and frantic.

I suspect Emerson would join me in saying that the rousing we all need comes not just out of slumber or lethargy. We need this awakening even in the times when we feel the world is demanding the most of us.

"Arise, shine," the prophet Isaiah tells us. What are the ways we might need to be awakened from the deceptive slumbers of this time of year in our schools? Advent asks us to think about this challenging but redemptive task. The good news is that we encounter, each day at school, a group of students that are crying out for that very awakening. They yearn for awakening; the question is, do we?

Shop, Shop, Shop!

December 10, 2012

Yesterday's *New York Times* carried a fascinating story about how the sheer inconvenience and frustration of holiday shopping—the crowds, cashiers placed in far-flung parts of the store, and the endless playing of Christmas Muzak (something annoying to a majority of the shopping public)—are not actually deterrents to shopping, as some might think.* In reality, the very inconvenience creates an over-stimulating environment that prompts a good many people to spend more, not less, money. It turns out the more uncomfortable you are, the more agitated you become, and the more likely you are to shop for more! Dissatisfaction leads to a temporary loss of control, making impulse buying all the more likely.

Apparently, in our efforts to want it all to go away, what psychologists call "cognitive closure," we are very likely to seek relief by spending. The writer even suggests that there is a part of us that actually enjoys being forced into the inconvenience, year after year!

The connection between over stimulation and impulse behavior is certainly a seasonal issue; after all, how many families' Christmas budgets go awry each year? However, it also raises for me the question about the highly stimulating environments we create for our students throughout the year. Could there be a link between impulsive, high-risk behavior and the high degree of stimulation and stress that we create in the lives of our students, whatever their age might be?

I am hardly a fan of making students feel comfortable all of the time. Our task is to help them work through discomfort as much as minimize it. But the degree to which expectations can come at our students from a variety of disconnected sources may create for them something akin to a holiday shopping buzz that can issue in a lack of impulse control.

It is telling that the author of the article suggests, in his conclusion, the need for a Buddhist-like sense of detachment from the frustration and frenzy of the commercialized Christmas world. As he put it, "Stand on a busy downtown street at dusk on a pre-Christmas Saturday...and decline to be swayed by the exhortations to spend, and suddenly it becomes an exhilarating experience."

If we are part of the problem of creating over-stimulating environments for our students, then we in Episcopal schools also have, at our disposal, a credible response to combating it! During this particular part of the year, it is, of course, called Advent!

---

*See, Oliver Burkeman, "Suffer. Spend. Repeat," *The New York Times* (December 9, 2012), SR1.

Beyond Words

December 17, 2012

I had just landed, on my flight to Washington, DC, on Friday, when I opened up my email and read the first news of the horrific events unfolding in Newtown, Connecticut. During the flight, I had been listening to a CD of Advent music, entitled, "December Stillness." Now a different type of December stillness descended upon our country: as we came to grips with yet another mass killing (we have been averaging one a month in 2012), there was very little to say. The raw and unthinkable tragedy of twenty children being killed in their school was something words could not help us capture or explain. On Friday night I watched TV newspeople struggling to find words—something they normally have plenty to offer—and our President having to pause for long moments while fighting back tears. No words do justice to our shock and empathy for those in suburban Connecticut, who now live with a loss and a collection of gruesome memories for the rest of their lives.

That such an event could occur during a season that celebrates children, peace among all people, and hope for the world was, of course, a very cruel irony. However, we need the message of Christmas all the more in face of what we have watched and heard. We are still a humanity that is capable of redemption, and we saw signs of redemption in the actions of those adults in the school on Friday: a school principal and psychologist who, having heard the initial shots being fired, ran toward the danger rather than away from it, and teachers who quickly and calmly brought their students to safe places. We need to hold on to those redemptive images as we live with a deep sense of grief and loss. Moreover, in lieu of words tossed around in the aftermath of this tragedy, some of which may seem trivial, we need to hold on to the Christmas message that so many of our schools will be hearing and celebrating this week, that Christ's birth embodies God's deep love for humanity and hope for our destiny.

Holding all of these things together, as we welcome back our children today for this last week of school, and then wishing them a happy vacation at the end of the week: that is our task. School may feel a little less safe this week, no matter how far away we might be from Newtown, Connecticut. But we are likely to find ourselves cherishing our students all the more, in tragedy's aftermath, and it is in school this week that our students in Episcopal schools will hear and feel the message of hope for the world that goes beyond all words.

Holy Dialogue

January 7, 2013

Like many of you, I was moved and inspired by the new movie, *Lincoln*. Surprised as well, I should add, by a number of things, including the high-pitched voice of Lincoln, as played by Daniel Day-Lewis. This is actually thought to be an accurate historical portrayal of his voice, but for some reason I was expecting a much lower tone (perhaps that says something about my assumption about how Lincoln's voice must have sounded!).

I was also surprised, in looking back on the film, how it was made up almost entirely of dialogue. The movie seemed to go from one conversation to the next, and some of Day-Lewis' most poignant portrayals of Lincoln occur when he is listening to someone else speak in a conversation.

It made me think of how the great Jewish theologian Martin Buber spoke of leadership in the Bible. Great biblical leaders rose or fell, according to Buber, not by making the right or wrong decisions but the degree to which they remained in dialogue with God. When the dialogue ended, the subsequent decisions of leaders reflected the fact that they were out of conversation with God.

At Christmas, God begins a new type of dialogue with human beings. It is a dialogue initiated by God, coming in an entirely new venue, where God not only interacts with humanity but takes on human form. It is a signal that God seeks a continual dialogue with humanity, one where both God and humanity are busy listening and speaking to each other. In Episcopal schools, it is the foundation and ultimate model for the value we give to the dialogue we engage in, wherever it may take place.

I wish all of you and your school communities a very Happy New Year, one that is filled with the holy fruits of dialogue!

Second Thoughts on Multitasking

January 14, 2013

Jacob Tomsky has worked for over a decade at the reservations desk of many hotels, and he recently published a very funny book on his experiences with guests, entitled *Heads in Beds*. Like many such "tell-alls" from the service and hospitality industry, this book pays a lot of attention to difficult customers. Here is what he says about one group that particularly annoys him, those people who go through the entire check-in process at the reservations desk while talking on their cell phones:

> Can you imagine how it feels, as a human, to be part of someone else's effort to multitask? While you say to the phone, "Uh-hhh. Yeah. Yeah"...I (at the check-in desk) get the lift of an eyebrow, side glances, brief and uninterested head nods thrown in my direction indicating your main focus remains on your call, perhaps a moment where you hold the phone slightly away from your ear to benevolently allow me 5 percent of your attention.

Whether it is the person we are sitting with at a restaurant, who patiently waits as we complete a telephone call, or the clerk in the supermarket, who gets the same amount of attention as Tomsky describes, as we text away, or the students who may intrude upon a task we are doing in our offices and who never really receives the full amount of attention they deserve, it is helpful for us to remind ourselves what it is like for the other person who ends up being part of our efforts to multitask. It is crucial for us to keep foremost in our minds what they are likely to feel, something it is so easy to overlook, as we get absorbed in the many things that occupy our lives.

I suspect we are talking not only about a matter of etiquette, but a profound theological truth, that the most important person God asks us to attend to, in the moment, is the person right in front of us. As Scott Brown, rector of St. Alban's Episcopal Church in Harlingen, Texas, told the new heads of the Southwest Association of Episcopal Schools in September, "God is here. The question is, are we?"

The Uncomfortable Goal

January 21, 2013

This past week I was reviewing a video on diversity produced by an independent school. As it began, one student in the video observed that diversity is a most unusual goal, in that, as she put, "The very diversity we aim for can, when it is realized, make us feel uncomfortable." Most of us know something about how difficult it can be to make a community truly more diverse; fewer of us have thought much about the fact that, once achieved, it may well issue in a more uncomfortable environment, far more challenging, in some cases uprooting, to everyone involved than the alternative of dwelling among like-minded people. It is indeed hard work not only making a school more diverse, but honoring it when there has been significant movement toward it. How many goals in life, I wonder, are pursued knowing that the end result may well be more uncomfortable than without it?

All the more important, it seems to me, that we hold on to the ideals—be they moral, theological, or pedagogical—that make the pursuit of a diverse community important. The difficult work it holds in store for us makes it all the more essential that we hold on to the reasons why we do it in the first place, helping to balance the many challenges with the conviction that this is the right thing to do. Of course, on a practical level, a more diverse community prepares our students for the global marketplace; it also helps our schools keep up with the good work our peer institutions are doing. So, too, it helps to celebrate diversity, not just work toward it. But these practical reasons are not enough. There has to be some type of ideal that reminds us that this is how our community should be. Indeed, this is how any community should be. That sense of rightness, of pursuing an ideal, which we attempt to carry with humility and grace, is what will keep us going.

That is why our yearly remembrance of Dr. Martin Luther King, Jr., is so vital to our efforts to build a more diverse community. In fact, it is more important than ever. More than anyone else, he was able to bring ideals to the hard work he undertook and which all of us, in our unique ways, hopefully continue. Without that vision, his movement would have perished, as all of our initiatives are destined to do if they are not accompanied by an overarching sense that this is what we should be doing. As we might say in Episcopal schools, this is God's work. That is what makes the hard work and the discomfort it may generate worthwhile.

Communication of Integrity

January 28, 2013

I recently finished Douglas Brinkley's biography of Walter Cronkite, who for decades was the TV news anchorperson so many Americans relied upon to give an honest and straightforward account of the day's news. His signature sign-off words, "And that's the way it is," served as a daily benchmark of being informed of what was important to know about the world.

At one point toward the end of the biography, Cronkite speculates on his long-term appeal to so many television viewers. He modestly explains it this way:

> There are better writers than me, better reporters, better speakers, better looking people, and better interviewers. I don't understand my appeal. It gets down to an unknown quality, maybe communication of integrity. I have a sense of mission.... I care about the world, about people, about the future. Maybe that comes across.

I don't know if your reaction upon reading those words was the same as mine, but I immediately thought of the great teachers in our schools, and the impact they have. For most of them, I suspect they—and we—might say that there are better scholars, better speakers, better organizers, even better looking teachers. But great teaching is about an unknown quality, and the degree to which a teacher connects with and inspires his or her students is something that can never be quantified. One thing we do know, I believe. It is about the communication of integrity, be it personal integrity, the dedication to young people, love of the subject matter, commitment to the school, caring about the future. All of these factors shout of integrity.

In his twilight years, Cronkite lamented the loss of that communication of integrity with the advent of the increasingly subjective and polarizing style of those who deliver the news to us. The type of unknown factor that Cronkite communicated to us may well be a thing of the past in the world of journalism. Fortunately, it has not been lost in the world of teaching. It is up to all of us in Episcopal schools to keep that precious factor at the forefront of our search for teachers as well as praise for those teachers who embody it.

At a memorial service held after Cronkite's death, President Obama described Cronkite's appeal and stature this way: "He invited us to believe in him. He never let us down." Isn't that what great teachers in our schools do each day? When it comes to communicating integrity, isn't that, truly, "the way it is?"

Those "Other Religious Schools"

February 4, 2013

During the past few months, I have been engaged in a book project, focusing on what religious schools in the United States—in all of their diversity and variety—tell us about the rapidly changing landscape of religious life in the United States.* It has been a fascinating and instructive project for me, and one of the lessons I have learned from the project is that many of those "other religious schools" we often tend to compare ourselves to turn out to be a lot more diverse than we might think.

In proclaiming our uniqueness as Episcopal schools, we are quite prone to speaking of what we are not, and among those "nots" we can all too easily refer to other religious schools and what we might assume to be their uniformity, homogeneity, and the presumed manner in which they force religious doctrine down the throats of students. After visiting Roman Catholic schools with majority non-Catholic student populations, or evangelical Christian schools where a majority of families do not necessarily buy into the religious mission of the school, or Islamic schools to which families send their children because they found no other type of school so diverse, I have come to understand that the pluralism we so prize in Episcopal schools is not our singular possession.

That does not mean, of course, that the manner in which we practice inclusion is not unique, or that Episcopal schools do not have a special role to play in the increasingly diverse and complex religious affiliations of Americans. It simply means that we need to be careful of how we speak about other schools, something I believe, on the whole, Episcopal schools have held up as an important value over the years. When we begin by saying, "Unlike other religious schools," we need to be aware of our tendency to stereotype and simplify them. If we look more closely, chances are that we will see in many of those schools a lot more openness to difference than we might expect, as well as a manner of teaching religion that does not match our assumption that they are imposing dogma upon unwilling or unknowing subjects. As with almost all segments of life, a second look will reveal much more, not less, complexity.

That reality may force us to do some re-thinking about how we talk about ourselves as Episcopal schools, but is that ever an unworthy enterprise?

*Daniel R. Heischman, *What Schools Teach Us about Religious Life* (New York, NY: Peter Lang, 2014).

Ash Wednesday's Dilemma

February 11, 2013

I always found the Ash Wednesday gospel to be such a challenge for students. Shortly before we began adorning our foreheads with ashes, in that penitential service, we would hear Jesus admonishing his disciples to be careful not to parade their piety in public. The disjuncture between what Jesus said and what we then proceeded to do was almost too much to endure, let alone attempt to explain to curious students who would approach me at the end of the service and ask, "Why do we put on ashes when Jesus has just told us not to?"

As many times as I tried, I was never able to come up with a satisfactory answer for them. The best I could do was reply, "Jesus is telling us never to take things at face value for granted."

This past week the results of the annual Freshman Survey were released. Each autumn, the survey is administered to almost 200,000 first-year students enrolled in colleges across the country, with the intention of finding out their views on virtually everything from study habits to religious beliefs to their hopes and dreams for what they wish to get out of college. Administered by the Higher Education Research Institute at UCLA, its results serve as a perennial barometer not only of the moods and values of new college students, but of the culture at large.

At first glance, this year's crop of students seems unusually clear and focused on the reasons why they are in college—to get a good job and earn a good salary. The percentage of students claiming these as the primary reasons for going to college is now at a record high: 88%. These students also appear to be confident: they believe they will be able to finish in four years (defying the trends) and view themselves to be above average in intelligence and leadership ability.

As Jesus warns us, however, things are not always what they appear to be. These confident, ambitious, and above-average students also reported the lowest rates of physical and emotional well-being since the surveys began asking such questions in 1985. About one third of students reported being overweight, almost half indicated high levels of stress, and 87% reported feeling overwhelmed at some point during the past year.

How can this be? Focused and hopeful students whose emotional and physical symptoms tell a very different story? I am not sure if my answer to students' questions were the best ones for their Ash Wednesday dilemma, but clearly Jesus' warning about taking the face value of things for granted is a timeless reminder about our human dilemma.

No Escape!

February 18, 2013

The gospel story of Jesus' temptation in the wilderness (the gospel for the First Sunday in Lent) is one of my favorites when it comes to preaching as well as listening to sermons. The one sermon I heard on the story that I remember most found the preacher reminding all of us that Jesus did not escape from reality by going into the wilderness. In fact, he told us, he was truly moving into a place that was quite real, not to mention challenging. Whatever we might be prone to categorize as one of the "escape clauses" in Christianity, this was not one of them!

I thought about that sermon twice in the past two weeks, after hearing comments made by Episcopal school people regarding the role that chapel played in the life of their schools. One comment came from a math teacher, who identified himself as an agnostic. Initially, he told me, he was quite reluctant about having to go to chapel on a regular basis. As he began to experience it, he grew to welcome the alternative vision of the school it provided. "It is something that we all do at the school at the same time, and we do it together," he explained. "We are all at the same level at that moment—with the students, with the head of school." Chapel turned out to be, for him, the great equalizer.

The second comment came from Hopie Jernigan, chaplain at

the Episcopal School of Jacksonville, the school that experienced the great tragedy of its school head being murdered last March. In the ensuing months, Hopie has played an invaluable role in ministering to that school community in the aftermath of that crisis. At the recent CSEE/NAES ChapToR conference in Tampa, Hopie told a most compelling story about her work over the past year. When it came to her description of the role that chapel has played, she told us, "Chapel was the place where it was never weird to bring things up."

Like Jesus going into the wilderness, chapel in our schools is hardly a place of escape. It is a place to which we go and encounter that which is most real—our common humanity, as well as feelings, convictions, hopes, and concerns that might not be able to find a home in any other corner of the school. Far from a retreat from all that is a part of the "real world," it addresses parts of that real world that may be hard to acknowledge elsewhere.

A Comeback for Moderation?

February 25, 2013

I was fascinated by an article by Frank Bruni, in the *New York Times* on February 10, 2013. Entitled, "The Land of the Binge," Bruni pointed to the seeming endless array of examples of how our culture is in love with the extreme. We go in for extreme sports, extreme partisanship, extreme eating and drinking. Even weather seems to be increasingly extreme! It is a supersized, over-worked world in which we find ourselves. Is it at all surprising, Bruni asks, that the percentage of voters who label themselves as moderate is shrinking, while viewers increasingly prefer to opt for either Fox News or MSNBC for their coverage of world events.

Bruni goes on to ask the following question:

Moderation? Remember that? It was once held up as an indis-putable virtue, virtually synonymous with prudence. Don't get too carried away with any one thing. Don't become too set in your ways. That was the message from parents and teachers. That was the cue the culture gave.

Recently I heard a group of chaplains give their take on what makes their schools truly "Episcopal." One of them spoke quite directly and proudly of the fact that we are a moderate tradition, steeped in the via media, be it between Catholic and Protestant or liberal and conservative. As I read Bruni's words, I thought about that description of Episcopalians representing a moderate tradition. In describing ourselves as a "middle way," we may well have something to offer to the world—a world that may find itself currently enamored with extremes, but a world that eventually may tire from overexertion and overstimulation, and actually be ready for a second look at moderation.

The Answer Is Local

March 4, 2013

I have just returned from the NAIS Conference in Philadelphia, where lots of people gathered to hear new ideas, explore pioneering visions for education, and learn how different schools do things in creative and compelling ways. Like our own Biennial Conference, these are some of the reasons why such an occasion—school people coming together to get a taste of the bigger picture—can be so valuable, not to mention a blessed change from routine this time of year.

In many of the workshops, attendees heard how individual schools do things, and the vast majority of that exposure to other models is energizing and thought-provoking. People left excited about the ways they might be able to apply what they have learned to their home turf.

At the same time, NAIS president-elect John Chubb offered us an important corollary to the process of looking for external models. As he told the association executives prior to the opening of the conference, "The key to the greatness of a school lies at that very site." The basics of an answer to an individual school's problems, or in its seeking to be greater than it currently is, are first found within the community, not outside of it. The solutions we are looking for are waiting for us within the community;

new ideas and new ways of doing things can only be made real by the people on location.

As the writer Margaret Wheatley once wrote, "There is no power for change greater than a community discovering what it cares about."* When a school community looks inside of itself for answers, it can explore potential new directions while reminding itself what it cares about, what makes its school community unique, and how a new initiative flows out of its very mission as a school. There is no greater joy to be found than discovering an answer to a vexing problem or a way out of a dilemma through looking within the school. There, within the realm of care about who we are, is where the best solutions are to be found.

---

*See, Margaret Wheatley, *Turning to One Another* (San Francisco: Berrett-Koehler Publishers, Inc., 2002), 48.

The Perfect Storm

March 11, 2013

Recently I visited a school where a senior student gave a power point presentation, in a school assembly, on plagiarism. Much of his presentation focused on the various dilemmas that student collaboration and use of the internet can pose in determining just what constitutes plagiarism today. What I found most fascinating, however, was his threefold explanation for why students cheat. It included:

- Fatigue (how many bad decisions do all of us make when we are tired?);
- Time (think of the many corners we are prone to cut when we are pressed for time);
- Academic pressure (whether that is self-imposed, parent-imposed, or—yes!—school-imposed).

To these three reasons I might add a fourth: being a young person! Whether it has to do with brain development or the risky behaviors so much a part of the growing up years, our students are going to make a lot of mistakes.

Together, these four factors create the perfect storm for plagiarism, and we have not yet even broached the topic of the presence or absence of personal integrity!

May I include a fifth reason to the storm? We teachers and administrators often do not take the time to stress, with our students, just why academic integrity is so important to us, both in terms of how it serves as a glue that holds together our profession, or the fact that it is hard to establish a climate of trust, in a classroom or in a school community, when people are cheating for whatever reasons. Sometimes I feel that we simply assume that students know why academic honesty is so vitally important to us. Given the frequent presence of fatigue, the absence of time, the pressure to succeed at whatever expense, and the propensity of young people to make mistakes, we need to be telling our students on a regular basis just how central honesty is to our understanding of what we do and why we do it. Academic integrity is not just about the way we do things, it genuinely means something to all of us who are dedicated to this education profession.

Episcopal schools are characterized by a deep pastoral care for students—including a compassionate understanding of why students make mistakes—but also by the opportunity to proclaim what is important to the adults in the community. If more of us shared our passion for honesty in the classroom, I suspect it might make a difference with at least a few students. Their knowing what it means to us may have a greater impact than we might first imagine.

Blessings

March 18, 2013

At a recent gathering of school chaplains from the Diocese of Southeast Florida, the conversation turned to the matter of blessings—be they the blessing of birthdays, animals, homes, or even automobiles! As the conversation continued, my sense of the role and potential impact of blessings expanded, particularly given the multiplicity of groups that we serve in Episcopal schools.

The Reverend Susan Keedy, head of school at All Angels in Miami Springs, Florida, talked about the wide variety of blessings done both inside and outside the school chapel, and the theological basis for doing them frequently and generously. "Blessings are free," she reminded us, "and there isn't anyone that does not want one." Moreover, "Blessings are common ground," they bring people together, she observed. They speak to key moments in peoples' lives, confirming the experience of receiving something, achieving something, and bestowing something. What's more, they are powerful confirmations of the great moments of transition in our lives.

As Samuel Wells, former dean of chapel at Duke University, reminds us in his book, *God's Companions*, a blessing helps to, "envelop the frailty of our lives with the embrace of grace." When we bless, we are reminded as well of our purpose as faithful people, to be a blessing. As with Abraham, through us others will be blessed (Gen. 12:3).

In a world where so many of our students and families are so geared to the future, blessings bring us back to the present, and remind us of what we have received in the past. They may well be an underutilized resource in the process of ministering to our school community, indeed bringing a much-needed sense of balance to those communities.

One thing I took away from the conversation with the chaplains that day: the next time I am asked to bless something, or the next occasion when I am blessing someone at the communion rail, as we so often do in so many of our school chapels, I will take it less for granted. People, young and old, bring so much to those moments of blessing, and we who do the blessing have an obligation to see these occasions as true moments of grace. Blessings turn out to be one of the ways we honor the wide variety of people we are privileged to serve and the depth and scope of the lives they lead.

The Many Sides of Celebration

March 25, 2013

As we enter Holy Week, Christians find themselves moving through a period of powerful and identity-shaping celebrations, from Palm Sunday through Holy Thursday and Good Friday into the joy of Easter.

The word "celebration" may seem quite fit for our Easter observances, but many might look suspiciously upon any of the other solemn events of this week as being, in any way, celebratory. After all, what is upbeat and uplifting about the more somber events preceding Easter? No wonder some may think twice about being a part of the earlier rites of the week, in favor of focusing just on Easter.

This may reflect our contemporary tendency to view celebration in a very limited fashion. Increasingly, "being celebratory" means whooping it up. That may be an important part of celebrating, but it is only one side. Our tendency to equate celebration with "whooping it up" reflects just how eclipsed the role of ritual has become in our culture. As the stage director and designer Peter Brook once observed, "We have lost all sense of ritual and ceremony…. We do not know how to celebrate, because we do not know what to celebrate." Brook goes on to explain that there are two climaxes of celebration: on the one hand, loud and wild applause, on the other, silence. Regarding the latter, "We have largely forgotten silence. It even embarrasses us."

Some of the events of Holy Week are designed to elicit silence from us. Some of them bring on joy and elation, even perhaps applause. Christ's presence is found in both, and together both of them point to the fact that we celebrate in many ways, from the very solemn to the very upbeat. That is one of the very extraordinary things about the Holy Week celebrations into which we are entering.

At a school I visited recently (not an Episcopal school, I should add), a faculty member who was an avowed, albeit regretful, agnostic echoed words I have heard from many serious, respectful, and, even reluctant, ex-Christians. "I miss the ritual," she freely admitted. In the absence of that ritual, I would guess she missed both types of celebration that make up the rich mosaic in our tradition. There is the type that speaks to one side of Holy Week—in all of its solemnity—and there is the type that gladfully awaits us at the other end of Holy Week.

Knowing When It's Time

April 8, 2013

Last week I was visiting Episcopal Collegiate School in Little Rock, Arkansas, and had the privilege—as I often do when visiting schools—of being at their daily chapel service. Students came into the chapel respectfully, keeping their conversations low and their demeanor modest. Then a moment came when all conversations came to a stop, and the focus was clearly on the worship service that was about to begin.

My assumption was that some signal had been made to students—whether it was the lighting of candles or someone standing up—to give them the sign that it was time to be quiet. It turns out that there was no such official signal. The community came to attention in a natural and quite un-self-conscious way. As Upper School Head Mary Lou Entzminger explained, this is how it is each day. There is no prompt. "They just know when it is time," she observed.

It may be the moment when we hope students will begin to focus on the occasion at hand; it may be the moment when it is time for them to speak up against an injustice or the bullying of another student; or it may be the point in their lives when they have to make a key life decision, such as whether to stay put or move on. Whatever the situation, one of the things we hope our students will gain is a growth in their understanding of "when it is time." That reading of the clock, that reading of an experience in life or what life is telling us is one of the "life skills' we most need in order to make respectful, courageous, and wise decisions.

In whatever context it might be, knowing when it is time is one of the greatest gifts that God can bestow on us. Episcopal schools can be and are indeed places where that knowledge can be cultivated.

Rediscovering Etiquette

April 15, 2013

When people today hear the word, "etiquette," many will think of something slightly outmoded, perhaps hierarchical, and even irrelevant to modern life. Images of the proper way to arrange a table setting, or how to dress for a particular occasion, may come to mind, and in an age of "casual dining" and "one style of dress fits all," those aspects of etiquette may seem highly outmoded.

I, for one, am a strong believer in etiquette, if for no other reason than the fact that it has to do with people more than place settings or proper dress. Moreover, I have seen how it can be effective: very few people do not respond warmly or positively to a "please" and "thank you," to allowing someone to proceed ahead of you, and—although it can make us feel old at times—to having someone say, "Yes, sir," or, "Yes, ma'am." It is both disarming and respectful, and, in our current situation, quite distinctive. It simply works for most people, and those who seek to practice it stand out.

Recently, I came across another definition of etiquette. Two authors referred to it as, "an ongoing self-awareness and awareness of others than puts people at ease rather than on edge."* Given the highly polarized rhetoric we hear each day, as well as the quite practical and moral problem that we see more and more people who do not seem to be able to talk with each other, that particular definition of etiquette carries immense contemporary relevance. What's more, the term is being used quite often in interreligious discussions today, particularly in how to be respectful and honoring of other religious traditions, whether in conversations or in being a "perfect stranger" in another, different house of worship.

The authors mention one more thing. Etiquette does not come naturally; indeed it goes against the grain of much of human inclination. We need to learn what offends, as well as what is welcoming. Sadly, but importantly, it is often up to schools to provide that sense of what offends and what is welcoming. At least we can remind ourselves, in the process of addressing these important and often neglected issues, that etiquette is not simply about the small social niceties, it is actually about meaningful global citizenship. It is about how we live with each other, and how we might be able to move beyond the current polarization to a welcoming starting point for greater mutual understanding.

---

*See, Douglas and Rhonda Hustedt Jacobsen, *No Longer Invisible: Religion in Higher Education* (New York: Oxford University Press, 2012), 74.

Something in Common

April 22, 2013

A few days ago I had the privilege of sitting in on a conversation that the chapel prefects at St. Paul's School in Concord, New Hampshire, held, regarding some of the strengths and challenges of the chapel program at their school. As with many other schools, there was high praise in that meeting for what these students regularly experience in chapel, including how they feel that chapel is a place where people are both honest and at their best as members of the school community.

I remember most a comment made by one student who said, "If you do not know someone (another student) well, and you want to start a conversation with that person, you can always talk about the day's chapel. At least you have that in common."

What that student was describing not only made good social sense—start a conversation about something you and the other person have in common—but also served as an important statement about the role of chapel in the life of an Episcopal school. In the midst of all of our diversity, activity, and varied pursuits, chapel is something we have in common. It is the constant. In a world of increasing specialization at an ever-earlier age, our schools still have something that regularly brings us together, that everyone is a part of and about which everyone in the community can talk—chapel. It binds us in community not only during the time we are gathered in chapel, but remains with us as a binding source throughout the school day, indeed beyond it.

I may be an artist and you are an athlete; I may come from one religious tradition and you from another; I may be a teacher and you are a student. Our schools are wonderful places of difference. That is what makes them such exceptional environments for learning. Still, you can always talk about the day's chapel. "At least you have that in common."

Being at Table

April 29, 2013

In the research I just completed for a book I am writing on religious private schools in the United States,* I have been interested to discover that one of the primary ways students speak about the quality of life at their school—i.e., whether or not their school community is a welcoming environment—has to do with whether or not students at that particular school would ever find themselves eating alone in the dining room. "We would never let that happen in our school," one student proudly concluded about the close-knit feeling of her school. "We would make certain that someone sat with that student." "If you are new here," a student at another school observed, "you will always find other students seeking you out and asking you to join them for lunch." More than any other way students described the culture of hospitality at their school, whether or not students could be found eating alone in the school dining room was the most frequent example mentioned.

I was reminded of this as I was reading Lillian Daniel's new book, *When "Being Spiritual But Not Religious" is Not Enough*. At one point in the book she concludes, "The desire to eat at a table with others seems to have been hardwired into human beings." There is something fundamental about eating and being with people at the same time. She goes on to observe that many people, when forced to eat alone, will watch television, or (as is often the case in the hotels where I stay, when I am on the road) will work on their iPhones while eating, simply because we human beings do not wish to eat alone. We need company, most likely because of the very nature of sitting at table.

This is something Jesus clearly understood. Some of his parables, as well as some of the most daring things he did in his ministry, had to do with sitting at table with others and eating with them. Table fellowship is vitally linked to the presence or absence of the Kingdom of God.

As we think about the quality of life in our schools, it is no small thing to be asking whether or not some students find themselves eating alone. All we need to do is remind ourselves of the last time we were in a situation where we were filling our tray for a meal in an unfamiliar setting, and were faced with the fear of where we would sit ourselves for that meal. Not a few of us, I suspect, worried in those moments whether or not we would find ourselves engaging with others. Young or old, to be human is to link our eating with others. It is no small symbol of what a community is or is not all about.

*Daniel R. Heischman, *What Schools Teach Us about Religious Life* (New York, NY: Peter Lang, 2014).

The Great Irony

May 6, 2013

It may be common knowledge that, in the hours after the Boston Marathon bombings three weeks ago, investigators were overwhelmed with thousands of still pictures and videos, pouring in via email and Twitter. These images came from individuals who hoped that, in some way, their pictorial accounts of what took place that afternoon might be helpful in tracking down the suspects. What may not be as commonly known was that another race was beginning to take place: officials were concerned to release official images of the suspects as quickly as possible to avoid chaos in the investigation.

Within a very short amount of time after the tragic event, thousands of individuals were going online and mimicking the official investigation. Amateur investigators were inspecting digital images of the crowd at the bombing site, and in some cases were coming to quick and irresponsible conclusions about people who might have been the bombers. The official investigators had to rush the release of the images of their alleged suspects, in part to limit any damage done to people who were being wrongly targeted as suspects on the Internet.

Increasingly we hear from school officials across the country about the added challenge, in times of school crises or controversies, of having to deal with what might be called a "side show" effect online, with quick judgments being made in social media about the situation in question, and, in some cases, individuals being targeted or preemptively accused. This obviously adds another layer of complexity—if not the potential for chaos—to what so often are already inherently complex issues.

Savvy school officials now need to be thinking about what may spin out of control online, when difficult issues surface in the life of the school. At the same time, this reminds us of the need to balance our technological advances with good judgment, patience, and a focus on interpersonal integrity. Thomas Friedman expressed it quite well in a recent column in the *New York Times*:

> ...the faster, more accessible, and ultramodern the Internet becomes, the more all the old-fashioned stuff matters: good judgment, respect for others who are different, and basic values of right and wrong. Those you can't download. They have to be uploaded, the old-fashioned way, by parents around the dinner table, by caring but demanding teachers at school, and by responsible spiritual leaders in a church, synagogue, temple or mosque.

Here is the great irony of our technological age: these advances do not render judgments of value and goodness any less important. They render them all the more important.

The Weariness Factor

May 13, 2013

During the past couple of weeks, school people from around the country have commented to me on one of the big ironies of this time of year: people on the outside assume that the school year is winding down. In reality, most people inside of our schools know it as the great "winding up" time of year! There is nothing like May for intensity and overloaded schedules, not to mention overloaded expectations!

One of the most helpful observations I have heard, over the many years I have worked in Episcopal schools, was offered by a veteran school head. "The worst leadership mistakes I have made," he explained, "came not because I had bad information, or did not know what I was doing. It had to do with making decisions too quickly, particularly making decisions when I was tired or overly stressed." My own experiences clearly resonate with that: there is a strong connection between being weary and arriving at poor decisions.

This means, in terms of decision-making, that this time of year is a vulnerable period for all of us. For much of the time this month we find ourselves running on fumes. We are expected to be many places at one time, the requests for decisions can stack up, and we may find ourselves trying to solve complex problems via email in the late evening hours. It is easy to find ourselves moving at such a pace that we do not realize the toll that weariness can take on our good judgment.

It reminds me of what Bob Johansen has consistently maintained. The increasingly complex issues that come across our desk these days necessitate more, not less, time for consideration and deliberation. But the demands of contemporary life pressure us, even more, into what he refers to as the "solve and run approach." Our natural mode of operation at pressured points in the school year does not equip us to work on the toughest matters we encounter (and how often they come in abundance this time of year!). Taking time to come to conclusion on weighty matters does not mean that we are being indecisive. It means we know that wisdom has a way of eluding us when we are weary.

Whit Monday

May 20, 2013

Today is "Whit Monday," as it has been traditionally known, the Monday after Pentecost, otherwise referred to as Whitsunday for so many centuries in the Anglican Church. In many Eastern Orthodox churches it has been known as the "Feast Day of the Holy Spirit," and in many contemporary church circles these celebrations around the Feast of Pentecost are referred to as the most underrated observances in the church year!

In his latest book,* Brian McLaren tells us that Pentecost teaches Christians two very important things regarding our faith as we live in a religiously pluralistic world. The first is that the Holy Spirit visited the early Christian disciples in a dramatic and unique way at Pentecost. We as Christians are the inheritors of this unparalleled gift of the Spirit as it blew through the house in Jerusalem. Second, by its nature the Holy Spirit is something that is ubiquitous—it is everywhere, and that means we Christians do not have the exclusive claim upon it. It manifests itself in the secular world, as well as in other religions.

From there McLaren reaches two important conclusions: we Christians can make claim to having received a real revelation of the Spirit in a very specific and distinctive way, which gives us something unique to offer to the world and to other religions.

It also means, however, that other religions, other places where the Spirit manifests itself have something to offer to us, based on their very real encounters with the Spirit.

For Episcopal schools these are, I believe, two important conclusions to be considering. In some cases, we do a very good job of emphasizing the first—what we have to offer to the world as Christians, while minimizing what we can learn of the Spirit from other religions. In other cases, we are very welcoming of and eager to learn from other religions, but more reticent to speak of what is unique and revelatory in Christianity. While the two may seem to be contradictory, we must hold them together. Pluralism in its contemporary form requires of us to be confident and genuine as Christians, believing we have something of substance to offer the world, while at the same time eager to learn from other religions, other sources that may well surprise us by their spiritual significance.

How is this "balance of the Holy Spirit" doing in your own school?

*Brian McLaren, *Why Did Jesus, Moses, the Buddha, and Mohammed Cross the Road?* (New York: Jericho Books, 2012).

The Year in Stone

June 3, 2013

Recently I had the occasion to visit a couple of schools where the possibility of putting the school's coat of arms, or their "core values," in stone was being considered, as part of the construction of a new facility. This prompted important discussions over whether or not the school really stood for the things those arms or core values indicated. After all, they were being etched in stone, with a lasting effect. Was the school truly serious about what was being said or depicted of them, soon to be on display for generations?

It led me to some thinking about the lasting effect of stone in a school, hence the questions I have for all of you, at the end of the school year, using stones as the principal image.

What were the milestones of the school year?

What were the key moments, the key achievements of this past year, which could be considered to be its milestones? What events helped to signify, in some way, that the school had reached an important new threshold in its life?

What were the millstones of the year?

If a millstone is considered to be something akin to a burden, or weight, what were the things that seemed to work against all of the accomplishments? What were the nagging issues, the things that weighed the school down with their persistent presence?

What are the cornerstones of the school?

In experiencing both the milestones as well as the millstones, what are the things the school keeps coming back to, as essential ingredients, the very things that lay at the foundation of the school's life and mission? In both the highs and lows, over the past school year, how were the cornerstones of the community present?

What are the stones that are about to shout?

In Luke 19:40, Jesus is asked by the Pharisees to silence his disciples, en route to his passion. Jesus' response is to say that the proclamation must take place; if the disciples did not speak of it, the very stones would shout. The phrase speaks of the inevitably of what is to take place, and how the story must be heard regardless of efforts to silence or ignore it. In turn, what are the issues from the school year that demand our attention, much as we might like to ignore them, that even the stones would shout out should no one put words to them?

These various "stones" may help us not only make sense of the year that is now concluding; they can become the building blocks for a stronger school community next year, something I very much wish for all of our schools.

2013-2014

Why We Come Back

August 19, 2013

You may have heard the story of the Ohio teacher who, last year, sued her former school, contending that she was discriminated against for having a phobia of young children. This particular teacher claimed she was fine teaching high schoolers, but when she was forced to teach 7th and 8th grade students, she suffered what she referred to as, "mental anguish," a sort that "no reasonable person could be expected to endure."

This may be categorized into the "truth is stranger than fiction" category, but it also drives home a basic truth about teaching: it is not the place to be, not the job to have, if you do not love young people.

Truly, what undergirds the excitement we might feel as we return to school, or even that sense of an impending, heavy weight of responsibility we are about to take on, all over again, is our fundamental love of young people. We teach out of that love for young people, it is the reason we do this work and the reason we have returned or will soon return.

As we greet our colleagues in gatherings and meetings prior to the beginning of school, and as we then greet our students as they return, we become reacquainted with and rejoice in that love that gives substance to what we do. There are few more poignant moments in life than those where we are reunited with our loves, and teachers are privileged to experience that reunification each year.

My predecessor, Peter Cheney, once remarked that, "You can't teach people to love children." It is truly a gift, a blessing from God, a sign of God's grace as we come together and make our Episcopal schools come alive, once again, alive with love.

Side By Side

August 26, 2013

There was a new voice, which you slowly recognized as your own, that kept you company as you strode deeper and deeper into the world, determined to do the only thing you could do—determined to save the only life you could save.

– Mary Oliver

You may know about the amazing natural phenomenon called, "The Wedding of the Waters." This is the place in the middle of the Amazon rain forest, some 1,500 miles up from the Atlantic Ocean, where two rivers—the very dark waters of the Rio Negro and the lighter-colored waters of the Amazon—flow side by side, 15-40 miles depending on the season. The two rivers travel alongside of each other without merging. Both rivers come from different places, travel at different speeds, and carry different temperatures. They play this extraordinary game of getting to know each other, and while they eventually wed, there is, in the words of one observer, "a long courtship."

The early weeks of the school year are, for a great many students and faculty, a time of courtship, of moving alongside the school and its culture, as each person considers whether or not the route he or she has chosen is the right one—what we like to talk about as "the right fit." This period of courtship may be conscious or unconscious, explicit or implicit. It is particularly the task of new students and faculty, but it can occur as a result of the changes that have taken place in an individual's life, young or old, prompting each one to ask if this particular school is the right place to be.

These considerations take time. As much as we hope each individual will find a home in our school, it is not something that can be forced or controlled. We simply honor that time period, that distance each one must travel before he or she is ready to merge with our particular school culture. We remind ourselves of the importance that difference makes in all of these considerations—be they differences of speed, background, or identity.

In this new ethos and environment, our hope is that individuals will recognize, in Mary Oliver's words, the new voices as their own. As they move deeper and deeper upstream, our hope is that a wedding of sorts will take place, that in the life of the school they have chosen each one will find there a way to "save the only life you can save."

It is not a hope that is unique to Episcopal schools, but one which comes naturally to our respective missions as places of hospitality, inclusivity, and the recognition of each person as a child of God.

Rising to the Occasion

September 3, 2013

Last week I had the unique opportunity to be present at the ordination of Joshua Hill at Episcopal School of Knoxville, Tennessee. Josh is the new chaplain at Episcopal School, and Bishop Young of East Tennessee ordained him to the priesthood in the school gymnasium, during the school day with the entire school community present, along with Josh's friends, family, and fellow priests from the diocese.

Two things struck me about this remarkable occasion.

The first is that, as unique as this was—as far as we know, it is only the third time that an ordination to the priesthood has taken place in a school where the ordinand was chaplain—there was something about that occasion that was far from unique. I refer to the response of students, who clearly and wonderfully rose to the occasion. Even the very youngest students knew and appreciated that something sacred was taking place. In a whole variety of ways these students honored the solemnity of the occasion, yet gave to that occasion a sense of joy, exuberance, and clear purpose.

These students rose to the occasion, in part because of what we instill in them in Episcopal schools, a sense of occasion, an awareness—cultivated through practices and patterns—that there are moments in our community life when we honor and respond in ways that the ethos and tone of the occasion require of us. Life demands of us not a "one size fits all" type of behavior for the various events we encounter. Whether in chapel, in how our students conduct themselves as representatives of the school in the community, or on school trips, our students develop an instinctive sense of what is expected of them at different times in their lives. This is no small thing.

Second, Josh mentioned in his personal remarks to the congregation, looking out over the assembled community, that he saw there traces of his life—his school teachers, his friends, his working colleagues—in that one place. Together, they formed a pattern in his life, a pattern that lead him to this moment.

Each of us is blessed with such traces in our lives—people who, together, form the pattern that has brought us to our particular places and positions in life. Together, they tell a story of our individual callings, whatever shape and direction those callings may be.

How blessed were those students, I thought, to hear someone speak of these traces in their life. Not only did they rise to the occasion that day, they were privileged to learn something of how people influence us, indeed lead us these occasions.

Be Not Anxious!

September 9, 2013

...knowing that thou art doing for them better things than we can desire or pray for.

> – Prayer for Those We Love,
> The Book of Common Prayer, 831.

This past week I was privileged to do some work with the faculty and board members of St. James School in Philadelphia. Now in its third year of existence, St. James is a member of our Episcopal Urban School Alliance. Seeing firsthand what has been accomplished there in a very short amount of time was—as is always the case with a visit to our EUSA schools—truly inspiring.

Our conversation that day had to do with the question, "What does it mean to be an Episcopal school?" In the midst of our discussion, the Reverend Sean Mullen, rector of St. Mark's Church in Philadelphia (the founding parish of St. James) gave his own interpretation of what being an Episcopal school, in part, means.

Father Mullen likened it to a "non-anxious" approach to questions of God and faith. On the one hand, he observed, we seek to be non-anxious about any urgency we might feel to make certain that our students "get religion" in one particular or exclusive way; such a task is done not by us but by God, in God's time. On the other hand, we are not anxious about and do not live in fear of the questions of God. Unlike our public or secular school counterparts, we don't avoid those questions, we welcome them, invite them, hopefully in a non-anxious manner.

In a world where questions of belief and religious practice seem so charged with anxiety—be it the fact that we might differ in our beliefs and practices, or that the question of God might be raised at all—it was refreshing to think about Episcopal schools offering a different way. The attitude Father Mullen so aptly described reflects an openness, generosity of spirit, sense of humor, and confidence that, I believe, characterizes the best of what Episcopal schools have to offer in terms of spiritual formation and welcoming of a variety of different voices.

To be sure, being "non-anxious" in the manner Father Mullen described is not easy—it requires a firm reliance upon grace (that it is not just up to us alone to accomplish our mission), as well as courage (that we do not sidestep the religious issues when they emerge or need to be addressed). It does not mean, as well, that we end up being cavalier or unintentional with what we are trying to do with our religious mission. When it is present, it does serve as an appealing and binding aspect of our culture and ethos as a school. People will be drawn to it as a refreshing change from a culture of religious anxiety.

Note: In last week's meditation, I mentioned that, to the best of my knowledge, the ordination at Episcopal School of Knoxville was only the third ordination of its kind at an Episcopal school. I heard a number of responses from chaplains who had been ordained at their schools in prior years. This is very good to know—thanks to all who expanded my knowledge pool! Fortunately, it does not take away from the unique character of that very ordination!

On Being an Adult, Part One

September 16, 2013

During our webinar for new chaplains, last week, the leader of the webinar, the Reverend Kirkland (Skully) Knight, middle school chaplain at Episcopal High School of Baton Rouge in Louisiana, made an observation based on something he remembered hearing from one of his mentors, the Reverend Bude Van Dyke, chaplain of St. Andrew's-Sewanee, Tennessee: young people are drawn to the oldest adult they know that takes them seriously.

There are many teachers in our schools who may have just returned to the classroom, studio, or playing fields wondering if they were up to the task, if indeed their energy and stamina could endure another school year—a year which is likely to be even busier than ever, if current trends continue. Some may wonder if they have lost touch with the generation they are teaching, that the various gaps—be it technology, attention span, or entitlement—are simply too great for an older person to overcome. Far better, some of them may think, for younger adults to take on the task of reaching and motivating students.

Chaplain Knight's words remind us that there is something of genuine value that maturity brings to a school community, something that transcends whatever perceived gaps there might be between one generation and another. It is a value that our students are searching for—the mature perspective—provided we take them seriously.

Taking them seriously, I would add, is not about mimicking student behaviors, preferences, humor, or language. Rather, it is about listening to their views of the world—their judgments, opinions, and questions—and seeing in them the potential for maturity. It is about allowing them to be serious human beings, for a change. That opportunity, in the lives of many young people, is all too rare.

The author, Ray Bradbury, was fond of saying that all of us—young and old—need people in our lives who can assure us, confirming that we are not crazy, that our struggles are genuine, and that we can be confident that we may in fact be on the right track. It takes a mature person to fill that role—where wisdom combines with experience—and it may well be that our students are seeking that from some of the very people that wonder, at times, if they have anything to offer young people.

On Being an Adult, Part Two

September 23, 2016

Over the past week I have encountered two tributes to teachers that tell us a great deal about what we, as educators, can provide for our students—things that teachers who also happen to be adults can offer to the young.

The first is a tribute to Paul Barrett, who recently retired from St. Albans School after nearly forty years of extraordinary service to that school—as teacher, college counselor, dean of faculty, and lastly as head of upper school (I would also add a most valued colleague of mine when I was at St. Albans). This comes from a former student of Mr. Barrett:

> Mr. Barrett's sense of humor, dry, quick, sharp but never harsh, has served, for more than a few of us, as a gateway to an adult way of looking at the world—adult, that is, in some utopia where grown-up people are possessed of intelligence, modesty, and lightheartedness in equal measure.*

The second comes from an article in the *New York Times Magazine*, which highlighted the brilliant career of Lou Volpe, longtime drama teacher at Truman High School in Levittown, Pennsylvania. The author, a former student of his who has just written a book on Volpe, shares one of the most remarkable things he encountered about his mentor, from so many of his other students:

> One thing I discovered…was that nearly everyone (former students) I talked to had the same experience I did with him. They felt at a certain moment, he knew them better than they knew themselves. That is what gifted, intuitive teachers do.**

Providing a window, through which students can glimpse an alternative mode of humor and humility, knowing students more than they know themselves: these are things that adults—and only adults—can do. We cannot underestimate what rare commodities these are in our world today. Daily, in Episcopal schools, we adults have the opportunity to offer our students a glimpse into what the grown-up world can be, and, in turn, offer a mirror to our students of what and who they are becoming as human beings. That is not just good teaching; that is the magic, if you will, of maturity.

*See, Alex Ross, "Mr. Barrett," *St. Albans Bulletin* (Summer 2013), 49.

**See, Michael Sokolove, "If All We Had Was a Bare Stage With One Light Bulb, We Could Still Do Theater," *The New York Times Magazine* (September 15, 2013), 39.

The Trophied Life

September 30, 2013

This past week the *New York Times* carried a fascinating editorial piece about the number of awards that children receive, both in and out of school.* The writer, Ashley Merryman, wrote of how trophies, once relatively rare objects to be bestowed, are now mass produced—trophy and award sales are a $3 billion-a-year business in the United States and Canada. Increasingly, trophies are likely to be handed out to more and more young people, in programs that give out awards to every child involved, even on frequent occasions.

Merryman's research, along with those of others, reveals that the proliferation of awards (what she calls "nonstop recognition"), originally thought to be vehicles of enhancing children's self-esteem and motivating them to do well, actually can cause them to underachieve. What's more, it can cause them to collapse at the first sign of difficulty. Thereafter, rather than experiencing that intense feeling of failure all over again, students are more prone than ever to cheat the next time around.

Are we doing our job of preparing young people, she asks, to face a world where they are likely to lose more often than win, where we need to learn from the many mistakes we make, as opposed to falling apart as a result of them?

In Episcopal schools, we have deep and compelling theological reasons for seeking to affirm all of our students—each one is a child of God. We also have a deep and compelling theological framework for those times when students stumble, make mistakes, and fail—we are finite beings, who consistently fall short of our expectations and hopes. God provides us a context for our failures, as well as an opportunity to learn from them and move on, blessed with God's forgiveness and mercy. We hold to both of these theological truths—sometimes in great tension, sometimes in wonderful balance as our students encounter and learn from the rough edges of life.

We should not confuse the belief that all of us are children of God with the need to be awarding all of the time. So, too, we should not, in the words of F. Scott Fitzgerald, confuse one defeat with final defeat. We have something more lasting in affirming children than what Merryman refers to as the "Trophy Industrial complex." But we also have something far more lasting than simply "learning from our mistakes," or, "learning how to lose." We have grace to proclaim, forgiveness to offer, and hope for a new beginning.

These theological profundities turn out to offer, for our trophy-saturated culture, some very practical and realistic value.

*See, Ashley Merryman, "Losing Is Good for You," *The New York Times* (September 25, 2013), A29.

God Is with Us

October 7, 2013

Many of you no doubt saw some or all of the television series on the Bible, this past year. As with so many media moments, this attempt to tell the story of scripture had its ups and downs: there were moving moments as well as moments that found me cringing.

Throughout the series, a common theme repeated itself in the words of assurance and hope from various biblical characters, "God is with us." Be they in times of joy or times of struggle and tragedy, the biblical characters repeated that refrain.

A particularly poignant moment in the series underscored the importance of this theme in negative fashion. Saul of Tarsus, prior to his conversion on the road to Damascus, is seen persecuting some Christians. In supposed triumph, Saul assures himself of the rightness of his actions by saying, "God is with me."

One of our greatest challenges in Episcopal schools, and what may also be one of the defining features of our being distinctively countercultural, is that we stress that "God is with us," as opposed to, "God is with me." Whether it is the worship we do together in chapel, in our serving others, or in building a community of diverse people, we are about the pathways of reaching God that enhance, rather than take away from, our common humanity. In a culture of so many "my's," we dare to stress the "we." Failure to do so issues in the self-righteousness and discord captured in that television moment featuring Saul.

Truly, we are about challenging a prevailing mindset that tears away at our common life. This we do in subtle, but persistent ways, reminding the members of our community that identity is not shaped by "going it alone," or that the group does not exist for the sake of meeting the individual's needs. As goes the common slogan of the University of Minnesota Marching Band: "The band does not become part of your life, you become a part of the band's life." In so doing, in whatever context, our individual identity does not diminish, but matures and flourishes.

Bishop Eugene Sutton, in writing to the people of the Episcopal Diocese of Maryland, spoke of it in this way:

> Unless we can get beyond the understanding that it is my family, my clan, my ethnic group, my race, and my nation that is most important to me, then there is no hope for the world in which we live, and there is no hope that we can grow individually into the people that we were created to be. (*Maryland Church News*, September 2013).

Only when God is with us is God with me.

Leaning Hard on "Episcopal"

October 14, 2013

At our most recent institute for heads new to Episcopal schools, held in Minneapolis, Bishop Brian Prior of the Episcopal Church in Minnesota challenged all of us not to shy away from speaking of and promoting our schools as being Episcopal schools. As Bishop Prior put it, "What if we lean hard on that word, 'Episcopal,' and see what we get out of it?"

I thought about the school head who might wince at such a suggestion. Would "leaning hard on that word" dissuade some families from considering our school, thinking that it was exclusively for Episcopalians? Would a stronger emphasis upon being an Episcopal school offend some constituencies (including some members of the faculty)? Would it raise difficult issues about religious differences and how to handle such conversations on difference within the life of the school? Isn't it better for families to discover the value of being an Episcopal school once they have enrolled their children, rather than, as we frequently put it these days, "lead with it?" Does this go against all of the conventional advice that marketing experts might give to schools?

As with any efforts to clarify our mission and identity, incorporating new images and language, or returning to reconsider more traditional ones, must be done with care and attention to the unique context of every school. What's more, in a culture where all religious terms—not the least, Episcopal—are easily misunderstood or unfamiliar, the task of interpreting and explaining this essential element of our school's mission is not going to be an easy or quickly appreciated task to undertake.

Still, Bishop Prior's challenge was designed not as an obstacle to be overcome as much as an opportunity we may be able to embrace. It presents itself as possibility, as a promising option that some of our schools may wish to consider. Dare I say that, given conventional and current cultural norms regarding what communities say about themselves, his suggestion was very much an "outside the box" proposition?

What would happen if, rather than shying—or, in some cases, running—away from that word, we actually leaned on it? What possibilities might it present? What avenues may open up? To be sure, we may not be used to revisiting such "old bones," but, as the prophet Ezekiel dared to have the vision to ask, "Can these old bones live?"

If we dare think outside of the box on this question we may just notice that not a few schools have done the same thing, and are proudly reporting some surprising results regarding what they got out of it.

Crisis to Crisis?

October 21, 2013

Like many of you, I watched in disbelief this past week as our nation came so perilously close to financial disarray, something we seemed to be almost willing upon ourselves. For me, it was less a matter of a partisan issue and more of an educational issue. As with every evolving story in the media, we teachers look at what is happening with a double lens: the first is our own reaction to what we see unfolding, the second is via the lurking question we inevitably ask, "What are our students learning from all of this?" What implicit "life lessons" are our students taking in, over which we can feel as if we have so little control?

I wonder what this most recent fiscal crisis has taught them and us about the common good. Has the notion slipped away from us, crowded out by partisan politics and concern for what is in it for me, or my position?

I wonder what has been taught, or not taught, about compromise to our young people. Again, has the notion quietly slipped out of sight, making us more vulnerable not only on the political front, but also on the relational front? As retired Maine Senator Olympia Snowe reminded us upon her departure from Congress, compromise and integrity are not mutually exclusive.

Lastly, I wonder if we are slipping into a "crisis to crisis" mode in our way of life, letting the immediacy of a crisis determine how we move ahead, as opposed to thinking ahead and planning for (and hopefully avoiding) what may happen. There is only one thing worse than what we experienced this past week, and that is the thought that it might happen all over again, come mid-January. Perhaps we spend so much time responding to crises these days—natural disasters, shootings, and unexpected world events—that I wonder if we have, without knowing it, adopted a crisis posture as our way of facing big issues.

On the positive side, it just may be that what we experienced this past week may remind us what we need to be emphasizing all the more in Episcopal schools—the value of the common good, the importance of compromise in all facets of life, and the need to be planning for and anticipating the problems we are likely to encounter in the future before we are staring them in the face at the last minute. If generations serve as a corrective force to their elders' foibles, perhaps the importance of what we are teaching our students in this vein may make our efforts all that more urgent and important.

Taking It Personally

October 28, 2013

Recently, at the annual meeting of the twelve-school Episcopal Urban School Alliance, we had a discussion about the types of qualities the leaders of these remarkable institutions look for in prospective faculty members. Part of our discussion focused on the need for teachers who, while engaged in the lives of the students they taught, were also able to rise above taking things personally. Students from all backgrounds, all socioeconomic levels, are bound to disappoint the teachers who are so committed to their growth and well-being. So can the adults in a teacher's life. The trick is not to let these disappointments sink in on a personal level. It reminded me of some advice I got from an upper school head as I was about to embark upon that same role. "I have three bits of advice for you," he told me. "First, don't take things personally; second, don't take things personally; third, don't take things personally."

This is the time of the year, I would contend, when disappointment can so often begin to enter into the life of a school community. Gone is the excitement and luster of a new academic year, and with it emerges the potential for people to let us down. High expectations collide with reality: people—be they students or adults—will not deliver in the ways we might have hoped or expected them to. The discouragement we feel over that reality has to do with how much we care for our students, colleagues, and school community, and the fact that our work is aspirational at heart—we want our schools to be places where the ideal is realized, where our missions are accomplished.

At its best, "not taking it personally" is not about having a thick skin nor a calloused demeanor as much as a realistic understanding of human nature—which is partly, I would say, a theological conclusion mixed along with some accumulated wisdom about how human beings operate. Being such an intensely people-oriented profession, we know many will disappoint us for a variety of reasons, and most of those reasons are not about us. We bring to our communities a rich mixture of motivations, rationales, and transferences; only a few of those really have to do with the person in front of us.

Because we care so much about the work we do and the people we serve, inevitably we will take some things personally. Ours is a profession with the potential for disappointment, even heartbreak. That is what makes the work so challenging, so engrossing. Perhaps not taking it personally is, in the end, a delicate matter of degree, of discovering the right balance of empathy and hope along with a critical distance.

The Heart of the Matter

November 4, 2013

In William Willimon's new novel, *Incorporation*, a well-established and forward-thinking Protestant congregation has just lost its longtime pastor, an individual whose single-minded focus on appearance as opposed to depth, over the years, had left his congregation expecting little in the way of theological substance. On the first Sunday the outgoing pastor is no longer in the pulpit, a retired minister announces to the stunned congregation the news of the pastor's departure. He then speaks to them simply and straightforwardly about the time of transition now upon them, while also putting a theological interpretation to what they were now and would be experiencing, something they had not been accustomed to hearing for quite some time.

Willimon describes the mood following the end of the pastor's sermon:

> The congregation sat in silence, stunned, overwhelmed, grateful.... Some of the flock wanted to applaud, but that didn't seem right. Others had a strange urge to weep but did not know why. Almost all knew that they had been led, in spite of themselves, close to the heart of the matter, the true point of it all.

As I read that description, I thought about such times in the lives of our schools. It may be found following a particularly poignant chapel talk, during a moment in a classroom discussion, or when news of individuals in the school community is shared in a meeting. At such moments truth seems to emerge with simplicity yet great depth, and those gathered feel themselves led to the true point of it all. Not surprisingly, silence is often our best response to what has taken place.

Many decades ago, I recall the silence in our college ethics class as our professor, who had just returned from a long illness, set his lecture notes aside and spoke to the class of the dual experiences he had encountered while being seriously ill: he felt he was not afraid of death, but also felt he had so much more to give in this life. What else could we do but sit there, stunned but also moved, armed with a sense that we had come powerfully close to the heart of the matter?

There are many ways our schools uncover truth, day after day. It may be through knowledge gained in the classroom, in the experience of defeat on the athletic field, or in the realization that hard work and determination pay off, either on an individual or group level. Another less frequent, but perhaps more lasting form, comes when news is announced or an experience is shared, and the gathered community feels being led close to the heart of the matter. We begin to understand that something powerful has occurred, and we sit in awe of the moment. A new path to God, to truth, has just been shown to us.

The Return of Laughter

This month marks the 50th anniversary of the assassination of President John F. Kennedy, and already it seems that there will be lots of focus on the president as well as the tragic events of November 22, 1963, and following. We are told that as many as 50 new books will join the existing 40,000 volumes already written about the man, his presidency, and the manner in which he died. No doubt new questions will also be raised about whether there was a conspiracy behind his death.

For those of us who remember that horrific day, it hardly seems as if it took place half a century ago, until we are reminded that most of our teaching colleagues were not alive back then!

As with the events of September 11, 2001, most of us living at that time can remember where we were when we heard the news from Dallas. Likewise, I so vividly recall how television news played such a central part in our family's life in 1963, as it did following 9/11.

Both events also shared a common question in their aftermath: when was it all right to laugh again? When was it "okay" to turn in part from the seriousness of those days to indulge in some lightheartedness? For the return of humor signaled the beginning of a return to life as normal, traumatized and grieving as we may still have been.

That question, "When it is all right to laugh?" is one that our schools encounter with great regularity. Just as Martin Luther was quoted as saying, "If you are not allowed to laugh in heaven, I don't want to go there," I think most of us would say that if we were not allowed to laugh at the many things that go on in school, we would not be in this business. At the same time, we also know how important it is to steer young people to the right kind of humor—the self-effacing and ironic as opposed to the victimizing type of humor—and that we are regularly faced with the question of how to react to the youthful humor we so often encounter that comes so close to the inappropriate: should I be laughing at this, or do I need to be severe?

All of this tells us that we cannot take humor for granted. It turns out to be, ironically, serious business. How it is used, when, and at whom it is aimed, are all things we need to be considering in our work with young people. As with so many things, our students need our guidance in determining when it is okay to laugh.

The Goldilocks Zone

November 18, 2013

Earlier this month we heard the news, from astronomers, that it is quite possible that there are billions of planets in the Milky Way that are just like the Earth, supporting life as our own planet does. In describing the conditions that need to exist on those planets for there to be life, the astronomers resorted to the familiar fairy-tale character, Goldilocks, to illuminate their descriptions: the planets must not be too big and not too small, not too hot and not too cold. As one writer put it, "they must be 'just right,' like the porridge, chair, and bed Goldilocks finds in the Three Bears' house."*

Have you noticed, recently, a growth in the number of occasions when writers and newscasters refer to Goldilocks? Along with the term, "sweet spot," her name is increasingly used to describe what might be called the "just right condition," a zone where a balance, a happy median, is discovered. Somewhere between the extremes of "too much this" and "too much that," we find Goldilocks being used to point the way to identifying that right, if not ideal, place.

Goldilocks being the intruder that she was, perhaps she is not the best model to carry us into a new sense of balance in our culture. Still, in a world torn apart, left virtually immobile, by polarization, images that help us capture a sense of moderation in the midst of extremes are sorely needed. One such image at our disposal has long been a hallmark of our Anglican tradition—the via media. As our schools find themselves responding in various ways to the extremes of culture, seeking to be reasoned, tempered places of learning and formation, the religious tradition that undergirds our schools can be a trusted ally, a long-lost friend.

What these images lack in the way of being provocative, like the attention-grabbing images of the two extremes, they more than make up for in helping us to discover what we most need, sustainability.

As the astronomers explained, we cannot have life without the right conditions, those found in a zone somewhere between the extremes. So, too, our schools, our culture, cannot find the abundant life we seek lurking at the edges of ideology or practice or in the crossfire between the two—we find it in the "just right conditions," where life is sustained and therefore holds the promise of thriving.

*See, Ben Zimmer, "Goldilocks, On Earth and In Outer Space," *The Wall Street Journal* (November 16-17, 2013).

Thank God, We're Free

Something very unusual occurs this week—our national observance of Thanksgiving and the Jewish festival of Chanukah coincide. This has not happened since 1888, and it is far from clear that the two celebrations will ever exactly coincide again. It is safe to say that it is the only time it will happen in our lifetime, so it is worth considering what we can learn when these two great observances converge.

I think about the fact that both holidays point to brave people who acted out of conviction. Behind the origins of both festivals we see people who were willing to endure great hardship for the sake of what they believed. If it were not for the Maccabean revolt, as well as the pilgrims braving an arduous journey, we would not have the freedoms we so often take for granted today. We owe our great blessing of freedom to those who acted out of conscience, indeed were willing to risk their lives for the freedom of that conscience.

Both festivals also give us an opportunity to experience freedom through the simple act of thanking God. As one writer puts it, Thanksgiving and Chanukah both point to the fact that by thanking God, we become free.* Thanking God becomes a moment when, no matter how bound we are by restriction, worry, or anxiety, we are able to rise above the here and now and find our ultimate freedom in God.

Perhaps that is why, through the years, one of the most amazing things I have learned about human beings is that many of the most thankful people I have ever encountered are those who have endured great hardship. So often, the words, "I am really a very fortunate person," come from someone who has faced great difficulty in life. It is not that these people are in deep denial, I would say, but they have found in their struggles a meaning to life and a way through acknowledging their blessings to triumph over those struggles.

It may be hard to imagine that by simply thanking God we may well be setting ourselves on a path to being free. We have the perfect opportunity to test out that assumption this week— Thanksgiving and Chanukah both encourage us to give it a try. It is a double opportunity. I would wager it will give us at least a brief moment of triumph over all that worries and restricts us.

*See, Tzvi Freeman, "Thanksgiving Meets Chanukah," chabad.org.

Unintended Consequences

December 2, 2013

When we hear the words, "unintended consequences," our tendency is to think about those outcomes that are not welcome, or those well-intended initiatives that create situations we had not anticipated and seem to backfire on us. While there are plenty of projects and efforts in the life of a school that produce such unwelcome surprises, there are also those that delight us, confirming that we are in fact doing something in Episcopal schools that is important and lasting.

The week before Thanksgiving I had the opportunity to be at Stuart Hall School in Staunton, Virginia. Following their middle and upper school chapel service, a very nice Thanksgiving meal was served to students and faculty at lunch. I was sitting with the head of school, Mark Eastham, at that lunch, when the student body president came up to Mark and asked if it was all right if the assembled group could call out the kitchen staff and offer its thanks, in this season of giving thanks, for all of the wonderful work they do each day for the school community.

Mark was delighted by the request, of course, but also—as were all of us at that table—quite moved by this gesture. No one had suggested to the study body president that this would be a nice idea. It came unanticipated, a gesture of thanks and respect generated—perhaps serendipitously—by the students themselves. But it was more than just a spur of the moment gesture: it also bore the mark of the school's influence on its students. It was confirmation that the sometimes tough day to day work we do with students, impressing upon them the importance of always considering how we treat each other, does indeed pay off in unexpected moments such as these. It was, to be sure, an unintended consequence, but one of those occasions which remind us that what we do with students can make a difference. Fortunately, every school has such moments; all we need to do is be aware of them (and give thanks) when they occur.

Advent is the perfect season to be recognizing these different types of unintended consequences, the ones that confirm to us the value of what we do in Episcopal schools. A persistent theme of this season into which we are entering is the affirmation that, if we are indeed ready to recognize the signs of God's presence in our lives, we will find them—perhaps on some occasions by surprise. All we need to do is be on the lookout!

Advent Advice

December 9, 2013

In a recent *Time* magazine article on boys,* Rosalind Wiseman makes reference to a dilemma that so many parents of boys have faced: "How do I break through boys' silence?" Reading this from the standpoint of being an upper school head at a boys' school for many years, I immediately thought of the many times I heard that question from a mother or father. For parents who wish to be close to their sons, seeking to keep the lines of communication open and active, there is nothing more disheartening than the frequent silence they might encounter from their sons when asked about the events of the day or the shape of their lives. It is probably the most frequent concern I heard from the many parents who shared their frustrations with me about how best to raise a boy in this culture.

Wiseman's advice was telling: try to avoid the constant questioning approach, particularly right after school. Boys, as a rule, tend to shut down in face of an intense round of questioning. Whether they are being asked to do something that makes them feel uncomfortable, or should they use silence as a tool of power, an open and effusive response to, "How was your day? or, "How was the test?" does not seem to be a common recourse. I wish I had known of that advice before I spoke with so many of the parents I worked with during those years!

Then Wiseman goes on to say something that is not only appropriate for helping boys to talk, it also struck me as pretty sound advice for the Advent season as a whole: say less, and allow for a connection to occur during quieter times. Just as boys are likely to say more when they are feeling more relaxed and less on the hot seat, so God reveals more when there are fewer forces at work for our attention. Whether it be boys saying what is on their minds and hearts, or God revealing some of the meaning of this Advent season to us amidst the noise and chaos of the holiday season, saying less and making room for quieter times may be just the way to keep all of us a touch more sane and expectant in the weeks ahead.

*See, Rosalind Wiseman, "What Boys Want," *Time* (December 2, 2013).

Finding God in Unlikely Places

December 16, 2013

Like so many of you, I found myself thinking a great deal, over this past week, about Nelson Mandela's life and witness. Particularly, I wondered about whatever transformation took place in Mandela's heart, during those horrible 27 years in prison. How could that experience prompt him to move in a direction of forgiveness, as opposed to callousness and a desire for revenge?

Perhaps the experience of standing for one's convictions, even paying the penalty for those convictions, served as a formative influence on Mandela. As he once reflected on his years in prison, "To go to prison because of your convictions and be prepared to suffer for what you believe in, is something worthwhile. It is an achievement for a man to do his duty on earth irrespective of the consequences."

However, it was a sermon I recently read that helped me to understand what may have been the most pivotal experience for Mandela in prison, an experience I heard little about during the week of intense media coverage following his death. On December 8, 2013, Chris Wilson, head of school at Esperanza Academy in Lawrence, Massachusetts, shared with the congregation at Christ Church, Andover, Massachusetts, about Mandela's teaching experience while in prison. After each day of hard physical labor, Mandela returned to his cell and thereafter taught other prisoners. As Chris described it:

> Mandela taught his cellmates how to read and write. They studied history. They learned math. They debated and learned to exercise critical thinking.... Nelson Mandela taught and his pupils listened. They studied and they learned. They made a place for God.... In that brutal, dark place, education was an essential gesture of hope.

Could it be, I wonder, in the activity of teaching that Mandela found hope, indeed, was able to develop a vision of forgiveness and unity for South Africa? Could it have been one of the key ingredients that allowed him to be the leader he turned out to be for his country and the world?

In part, this is something we all do in our vocation as educators. In some of the most unlikely of places, we create hope. We make a space for God, and in so doing we change not only our students but change ourselves.

One of the core messages of Christmas is that God is to be found in the most unlikely of places. Imagine Nelson Mandela teaching in prison, creating hope in a place where so little of it could be found. As with Bethlehem, there is where we find God.

The Other End of Resolutions

January 6, 2014

Elie Wiesel once observed that God's greatest gift to humankind was not that God created us, but that God granted us the ability to be able to begin again. As he writes:

> Therein lies the beauty and the grandeur of the Jewish tradition: every human being is granted one more chance, one more opportunity, to start his (or her) life all over again. Just as God has the power to begin, man has the power to continue by beginning again—and again.*

No doubt you have noticed how our culture, at this particular point and time in the calendar, is awash with talk about and helpful tips on resolutions for the new year. Whether we are joining a health club, changing our eating patterns, or being more patient, it is resolution time. We seek a marriage of desire and will, and the new year offers us an inbuilt beginning, an inherent optimism about what can be done.

Many of our students who return to school following the holiday break come infused with a sense of resolve—to do better in school, change old habits, or in some cases actually seek to be an entirely new person. What do we do and say in response to them—as well as to ourselves—as we seek to begin anew?

Certainly we should encourage them, find ways of holding them (and ourselves) accountable, and help shape those big dreams into feasible, attainable goals. But we can also speak of the unspeakable, those moments when resolve begins to weaken, or actually falls apart. These are the times that will no doubt lie ahead for so many at the other end of their new year's resolutions. For such moments we can tell them—and ourselves—of the gift that God has given us, to begin again and again. Nothing worth doing in life is failure-proof, above worth trying again and again. As Mary Pickford observed, "What we call failure is not the falling down, but the staying down." When the crunch of time or the passage of time begins to eat away at our resolutions, we can speak of a hope that allows us to keep going.

You may remember what Winston Churchill once said: "Success consists of going from failure to failure without loss of enthusiasm." That "enthusiasm" of which he speaks, in our framework of meaning, is about the hope and the opportunity that awaits us when it is time to begin yet again.

---

*Elie Wiesel, *Five Biblical Portraits* (Notre Dame, IN: University of Notre Dame Press, 1981), 151.

Facing Cold Winds

January 13, 2014

In an address before the United Nations Press Corps, in December of 1959, UN Secretary-General Dag Hammarskjöld observed, "I think we should face the cold winds of the day." Hammarskjöld's exhortation also turned out to be prophetic—with situations in the Middle East, Laos, Tibet, and the Congo awaiting him in the year that was to follow, the cold winds were about to test him, not to mention the role of the UN, like never before.

Over the past week, many of us in a large part of the country were indeed facing cold winds—temperatures and wind chills that many had not experienced in their lifetimes. A chilling time, to put it mildly. School cancellations, and all of the attendant complications, abounded, as did problems with heating and plumbing. Many teachers and administrators found themselves reminding families of the some of the most fundamental needs to prepare children for the unprecedented cold weather.

Of course, Hammarskjöld's reference to cold winds was of the metaphorical variety, and this time of year brings to schools its own share of those types of winds as well—tough matters that we are all too inclined to sidestep but we know in our hearts need to be addressed. So, too, they are often cold winds that come (as they did with the weather last week!) in multiples.

Hammarskjöld was a model of courage and grace under fire, as he faced the cold winds of 1960. Quietly, deliberately, with an eye to the basic mission of the UN, he carried out his duties. But he also reminds us of the hope and redemption that comes when we do face those cold winds, for our lives are defined not by what we have avoided, but by what we have addressed. As he wrote in another instance, the dirt and grime of life also turns out to be "the ground from which the flame ascends straight upwards."

Someone asked me, last week, about the times in my work when I felt I had handled difficult personnel situations well. My response was that, in retrospect, I never felt I handled them well, due to the delicate and complicated nature of each situation, as well as the fact that I was always aware of how individual lives were being impacted by the decisions I made. If I could say, in retrospect, that how I handled them forwarded the best interests of the institution I was serving, then that would do.

So may we hope we face the cold winds with courage and grace, knowing that we seek to act in ways that serve the good of our schools.

Out of Character

January 20, 2014

On Easter Day in 1961 readers of the *Saturday Evening Post* were surprised by a Norman Rockwell painting on the cover of the magazine. It was unlike any *Post* cover painting Rockwell had done in years past. The seeming champion and chronicler of traditional American values had put together a mosaic of people from many cultures, nations, and religions. Superimposed on the painting were the words of the Golden Rule. On the bottom left of the painting was an African-American schoolgirl, dressed in white blouse and plaid jumper, glancing at the viewer. Her presence in the painting points to what would be a common subject in Rockwell's paintings in the years ahead, the battle for school desegregation.

Viewers of the painting in 2014 may take such a mosaic for granted. However, one cannot overestimate the controversy it stirred at the time of its publication. Portrayals of different races in the same place, presented as social equals, were rare at this time. It was, in the words of Rockwell's biographer, "A love-thy-neighbor manifesto in paint."*

What prompted Rockwell, known heretofore for his depictions of the common lives of white Americans, to take on such a subject, indeed to take such a risk with his subject matter? Was he influenced by the studying he was doing of world religions? Had he seen evidence of injustice with his own eyes? Had he been in any way influenced by his mentor, Erik Erikson, who spoke often of the importance of the Golden Rule? Had the words and example of Dr. Martin Luther King, Jr., or John F. Kennedy stirred him?

Whatever the reason, Rockwell's *The Golden Rule* seemed very much out of character. Yet it did signal a major change in his work, perhaps even the beginning of his estrangement from the *Post*.

But evidence of injustice, or the inspiration of those who point to and beyond injustice, can do that to us—it can cause us to do things that may seem out of character. Rockwell stands as an example of one who began to read the needs and tones of the times, and allowed those times to have an impact on him. We see such examples of this so often in our schools. Through first-hand acquaintance with someone who has experienced injustice, or through the knowledge gained in studying a subject, lives can truly change.

We pray, on this day when we celebrate Dr. Martin Luther King, Jr., that we might be alert to the cries of our times, and respond in ways that will bring people together under common values, such as Rockwell's painting so profoundly depicted.

*See, Deborah Solomon, *American Mirror: The Life and Art of Norman Rockwell* (New York: Farrar, Straus and Giroux, 2013), 340-343.

Hope for the Future

January 27, 2014

A curious but positive thing seems to be happening to me as I progress in years: more and more I find myself thinking about the future, and much of it has to do with a future well beyond my own lifetime. Never before in my life—even in those times when, as a young person, I was always obsessing about the next steps in life—has the future been of such urgency to me. As I ponder the future shape of our schools and churches, including the issue of where we will find the good people to lead them, I find myself feeling passionate about a world that I am not likely to see.

It is, of course, not entirely altruistic, as one of my central concerns is whether or not the values that I cherish will endure. Inevitably, if you feel strongly about something, you want to see the future reflecting it, even resolving it.

The future was very much on my mind and heart as the NAES Governing Board met in Haiti, this past week. All around us, the future was on display, in dramatic and at times deeply moving ways. I recall how the Reverend Margarette Saintliver, who ministers at Church of the Transfiguration, Gorman, and directs its school, so inspired us by her vision for what the school was about and the example she so clearly sets for many young women eager to serve the church in Haiti. She spoke of her view of education as an extension of the very name of her parish, transfiguration.

I recall the excitement and sense of mission that radiated from the seventh and eighth grade students we met from All Saints' Episcopal Day School in Phoenix, who spoke about the trip to their partner school and church that they were just completing. There was a confidence and sense of deep satisfaction in how they spoke about their week in Haiti—clearly they felt they had a part in helping to shape the future in a very tangible way.

Then there were the students we saw every morning in Port-au-Prince, walking to school. They were visible by their school uniforms—I stopped counting the different uniforms I saw one morning when I reached 50! Amidst the throngs of people who crowded the city streets, they stood out not only because of what they were wearing, but as visible symbols of hope for Haiti's future.

Our work as educators is very much about creating hope for the future. How blessed we are by that; how blessed we were by these young people of Haiti, and those committed to them, who reminded us once again of our hopeful mission.

Underrated Forms of Communication

February 3, 2014

In their new book, *Healthy Schools: The Hidden Component of Teaching and Learning,** Phyllis Gimbel and Lenesa Leana talk about some of the most common problems that faculty members point to when they speak of what makes their work frustrating. Having no time to talk about what is important to them is among the most frequent. Another has to do with the consistency with which rules are enforced and expectations made clear. Still another is the lack of sufficient communication with faculty.

Sound familiar? I suspect these three concerns are echoed in the frustrations expressed by a great many teachers in our schools: time, consistency, and communication!

Regarding that third concern, Gimbel and Leana make a very significant point. Communication is not only about speaking or writing, getting the word out, and sharing information in verbal or written form; it is often, they remind us, also about listening. In fact, listening may well be the most underrated element of communication in a school. Our natural tendency is to assume that when a perceived lack of communication is identified, it has to do with something not being expressed. The administration has not been talking or writing enough! Gimbel and Leana point out that it is often to do with the feeling of not being heard. How school leaders care for their faculty is of greater concern to these faculty members than how the school is managed, they tell us, and one of the surest signs of that care is the sense faculty have that they are being listened to and understood.

To be sure, being heard and understood is not the same thing as having one's way. Good listeners who happen to be school leaders know, however, that if a faculty feels heard in the process of making a decision, the outcome, whatever it may be, is likely to be more acceptable.

The next time we hear a concern about communication, perhaps we should withstand the temptation, in response, to say or write even more. Perhaps it is less about communicating to faculty and more about communicating with faculty. Communicating with others always includes the component of listening. That concern about the lack of communication may well have to do less with the lack of being told about something than the lack of being heard.

*Phyllis Gimbel and Lenesa Leana, *Healthy Schools: The Hidden Component of Teaching and Learning* (New York: Rowan and Littlefield, 2013).

On the Front Lines

February 10, 2014

In a recent article, columnist David Brooks referred to what he called a "strong vein of hostility" against religion, and even religious believers, in our country today, particularly among the young.* As Brooks wrote, "When secular people are asked by researchers to give their impression of the devoutly faithful, whether Jewish, Christian, or other, the words that come up commonly include 'judgmental,' 'hypocritical,' 'old fashioned,' and 'out of touch.'" This led Brooks to conclude that many believers experience a gap between their experience of faith and the cultural perceptions of what that faith is about. Little wonder, then, that many believers are quick to stress just how nonjudgmental and accepting they really are, or, as I found in the interviews I had last year with school parents, a lot of people will tell you that they are Christian but are quick to appendage that with, "But I am not...."

It is important to emphasize that not all secular people or "none of the above" segments of our population express such hostility. Likewise, religious institutions have given the secular world more than enough reasons why to be wary of us. Still, we are left so often with a sense that many today regard us with some degree of suspicion.

Brooks' conclusion comes as no surprise to those who lead or minister in Episcopal schools. We are familiar with the various symptoms of what might be called religious hostility, such as parents of prospective students who express concern over the religious mission of the school, including the fear of indoctrination in the classroom or chapel.

At our chaplains' conference, this past weekend in New Orleans, Professor Lauren Winner of Duke Divinity School shared with our chaplains some of the learnings she has gleaned from her time as an interim chaplain at St. Mary's School in Raleigh. One of those learnings is that school chaplains are, in her words, "the shock troops of what the church at large is worried about," in terms of relating to a culture so skeptical about religious belief. School chaplains are on the front lines in facing cultural worries and misimpressions about what we do religiously in our schools.

What strikes me is how gracefully and calmly our school chaplains deal with being on these front lines. So often, they come to the aid of a teacher or admissions officer who has encountered a questioning parent. What's more, by their sheer presence they so often convey an assurance to those inside and outside of the school that we are not up to rigid, overbearing antics when we take seriously being an Episcopal school. For that alone our chaplains deserve our thanks.

*See, David Brooks, "Alone, Yet Not Alone," *The New York Times* (January 28, 2014), A21.

Where's the Bible?

February 17, 2014

In a *Wall Street Journal* article,* prior to Presidents Day, Tevi Troy focused on the relationship of the Bible to presidents throughout American history. One fact he shared was that, until the 1970s, Air Force One did not have a Bible on board. Obviously, this created a problem on November 22, 1963, given that Vice President Johnson was to take the oath of office on board en route back to Washington, DC. There was no Bible to be found! It turned out that Johnson took the oath of office with his hand on a Roman Catholic missal, the Catholic equivalent, you might say, of our Book of Common Prayer. Subsequent presidents requested that a copy always be on board.

Not having a Bible around, but being able to find a liturgical book: that sounds, for better or worse, characteristically Episcopalian! It led me to think about the place of the Bible in our Episcopal schools. For many of our schools, I believe it is akin to a companion in worship, study, and a source of inspiration for key events in the life of the school community. For others, it is something that mostly rests on the shelf, occasionally alluded to in literature or history classes, but hardly a living document. For others, it is a source of serious study in religious studies classes. For some, perhaps the Bible is off-limits, echoing the situation a few weeks ago when a Michigan public school banned an 8-year old boy from bringing his Bible to class—he claimed enjoying reading the Bible during his free time. As school officials explained, the book was "only for church, not for school" (the decision was subsequently reversed!). It may also be an embarrassing, awkward document: what do we do with it in an age of great religious pluralism? Still, for others, it may be—like Air Force One in the 1960s—something very hard to find!

What is the place of the Bible in your school? That is hardly an antiquated question, or one that is the exclusive domain of conservative evangelical Christians. Is it something visible, audible, in the life of the school? Moreover, is it seen as something lively and challenging, not just a fragment from a more homogenous religious past but something which actually helps in the efforts we make to be inclusive? As Troy quotes President Obama, from his book, *The Audacity of Hope*, "When I read the Bible, I do so with the belief that it is not a static text but the Living Word and that I must continually be open to new revelations—whether they come from a lesbian friend or a doctor opposed to abortion."

*See, Tevi Troy, "The Presidential Bible Class," *The Wall Street Journal* (February 14, 2014).

Recalling Our Goals

February 24, 2014

One of the trickiest parts of this particular time of the year in schools is that, on the one hand, there is so much to do in the present moment, while at the same time we are busily—sometimes frantically—making preparations for next year, whether in admissions, hiring, or finalizing budgets. We are living through an intense part of one year while highly involved in planning for the next. What might be most at risk in this type of situation? I would say the goals that we set out for ourselves at the very beginning of the year!

It may seem a long time ago, and it may feel as if we have travelled a million miles in record time since August or September, but I would guess that most of us set out some goals back then for the year, and that we may well have lost track of at least a few of them somewhere along the line. What would it be like, at this juncture, to go back and review those goals, as individuals, as administrative teams, or departments? What might we be surprised to find, or find ourselves reminded of, by taking those goals off of the shelf, dusting them off, and daring to take a look at them?

In a chapel talk he gave in November,* Groton School student Henry Barker recalls how, at the beginning of his Fifth Form (junior year) English class, his teacher asked the students in that class to write down their goals for the year. The teacher then collected and saved those goals. As time passed, Henry had forgotten about those goals, and was surprised to find, at the beginning of the following year, that very list in his mailbox. What's more, he was surprised to see how the passing of time had altered his goals: what seemed to have top priority entering into that previous year no longer meant that much now.

What if the goals we had set out for ourselves at the beginning of this school year all of a sudden reappeared in our mailbox at school? What would we see there, and what are the types of things we had written down that we may have well forgotten about with the passing of time? Furthermore, how has time altered our sense of priorities?

Then comes the really big question: how might reviewing our goals for the year, at this particular time of the year, make a difference in the quality and tone of the next few—admittedly very intense—months?

*See, Henry Barker, "Patiently Looking for Meaning," *Groton School Quarterly* (Winter 2014).

What's Next?

March 3, 2014

At our Early Childhood Education day, last week at St. Paul's Episcopal Church and Day School in Delray Beach, Florida, I began the program by asking registrants to introduce themselves and, in doing so, to offer at least one question or concern they brought with them to this day. One educator came with a very simple question regarding her school: as she put it, "What's next?"

All of us can ask that question of ourselves and of our schools—"What's next?" The context of that question might be an immediate one. With the flurry of activities that fill up our lives this time of year, we may be wondering what next, on that long list of things to be done, needs to be attended to. In a vein similar to that of a harried salesperson, we may find ourselves yelling out, "Next." Likewise, with the number of problems that can attend this time of year, we may wonder in exasperation, "What's next?" What other problem situations or difficult people now need our attention?

On a larger scale, the question may have to do with the next big initiative, or the next big decision, the school will encounter. Do we face challenges in the way we respond to changing demographics, changing enrollment patterns, or financial sustainability? Do we need to address the impact that such changes may have on a school culture we have come to love? Do we have important decisions ahead of us regarding our relationship to our Episcopal identity?

The question can also be asked in the context of considering the unpredictable or unintended. What is next in terms of surprises that may have an impact on our school community? One thing I believe we can all assume, given the events of the past few years, is that as carefully we plan for something going wrong, there is always something unanticipated potentially lurking around the corner that can catch us off guard. After all, real life is stranger, and more surprising, than fiction!

"What's next?"—a question we find ourselves asking a lot in school, on a number of different levels. The level at which we are considering that question can say a great deal about the time of the year as well as the mood and level of morale that we experience.

As educators in Episcopal schools, we can ask that question with a degree of confidence, not just worry or panic, knowing that God will be with us and guide us in meeting up with whatever is next. As one person recently put it, "When God acts, it is always surprising." Fortunately, as well, God always provides us the compassion and strength to meet those surprises.

Ash Wednesday Controversies

March 10, 2014

Last year the big controversy surrounding Ash Wednesday had to do with the practice of some churches doing "Drive-by ashes," where hurried passers-by could stop their cars, poke their heads out the window, receive ashes on their foreheads, and move along. This year it was the practice of "Ash Wednesday selfies."* After some individuals had received ashes, they would group together, take a picture of themselves with ashes on their foreheads, and post it on social media.

Supporters of the selfie trend on Ash Wednesday argued that the end justified the means. "Any way we can encourage people thinking about their faith, their spirituality, we want to do that," one Catholic priest explained. Opponents contended that the very practice of taking a selfie was antithetical to the nature of the observance. "Selfies themselves are narcissistic," said one theologian. "That is exactly what Ash Wednesday is supposed to be conquering."

As with many issues connected to technology and social media, this one can generate a lot of feeling, both pro and con. Rather than lay the blame on iPhones and Facebook, perhaps the words of one school technology director are worth repeating: "Technology is merely a stage upon which the human drama is most prominently acted out today."

So, too, I wonder if there is something about the very nature of penitential days and seasons, such as Ash Wednesday and Lent, that makes our culture feel uncomfortable. If we are more and more about promoting ourselves, how then does repentance and self-denial mesh with contemporary values?

Lastly, I wonder about the comment that any way that gets people thinking about faith and spirituality is a good thing. Any way?

While no doubt there are many who would claim that Episcopal schools are institutions that are drifting away from tradition, I continue to be impressed by the degree to which our schools take the liturgical traditions of the Episcopal Church seriously, in some cases more seriously than some segments of the Church. In so many schools these traditions live in balance with the wide variety of people and beliefs that are found in those schools.

I was honored to be present for Ash Wednesday services at St. Martin's Episcopal School in Atlanta, last week. Surely, the imposition of ashes was something unfamiliar to many students. Yet the observance was explained carefully and disarmingly by the chaplain, and while many chose not to receive ashes, there was a clear sense that something holy was taking place. Tradition was honored, even in the midst of a religiously diverse, contemporary student body.

This was not simply any way, but a way of real spiritual substance.

---

*See, Ben Kesling, "Selfies Bring Ashtags to Lent," *The Wall Street Journal* (March 6, 2014).

The Look

March 17, 2014

In a recent dinner conversation, a group of us were reminiscing about some of our favorite and most influential teachers, and one of the common features identified in so many of those mentioned was something referred to as, "the look." This was the capacity of these teachers to induce a sense of calm, seriousness, or moral accountability among their students simply by looking at them in a certain way. In essence, when a particular teacher conveyed a look, his or her students knew the time had come to re-focus, settle down, or discontinue whatever they were doing. All it took was the infamous "look," and the mood and tone changed. Nothing else was needed.

At first glance, it might be tempting to think that "the look" was simply a skill that a teacher had been able to develop, like a technique. Tilt one's head, squint ever so slightly, and peer into the group of students without staring directly at any one of them, and there one had it—the look! That, however, would only be a superficial rendering of what the look was about, let alone its impact.

"The look" came from teachers we students grew to respect, from teachers whose integrity was so transparent that it was likely that we could imagine what they were thinking without ever hearing them say a word. These were people who stood for something, and in turn expected much from their students. As students we came to know the look from our experience with these teachers, and we did not wish to disappoint them by virtue of the admiration we had grown to have for them. They did not attempt to be our friends or buddies, but kept a compassionate, adult distance from us. But we still knew who they were, nonetheless.

Like so many things we remember about our favorite teachers, "the look" is predicated upon our understanding of and appreciation for them as role models and voices of integrity. The words they spoke, the actions they took, even the eccentricities which endeared them to us, would not be recalled to this day if it were not for the foundation upon which they rested—what these teachers stood for and expected from us.

Far from being a technique, "the look" stood for something far deeper in these teachers. It served as a window into their soul.

A Sign of Permanence

March 24, 2014

Recently I read one observation from *New York Times* writer Dan Brooks that made the most sense to me of anything I have encountered about our contemporary—and, to me, mystifying—fixation with tattoos. In a world of great instability, he explained, where very few things feel lasting and stable, many are drawn to tattoos as one of the few marks of permanence in their lives. At first glance, the fact that tattoos are "for keeps" may seem like a discouragement to those who might wish to have them adorning their bodies. After all, how will people feel about these lasting marks of youth as they move into middle age? On the other hand, what other things in life carry as much tangible certainty as tattoos?

Recently, in the monthly newsletter of Independent School Management,* I came across these words: "While continuity was a 20th century staple, unpredictability is today's watchword." I am not entirely certain that continuity was a hallmark of the previous century, but it is pretty clear from most indicators that what the writers are saying about our current "watchword" is right on target. People, institutions, and values can all too easily exude a sense of transiency and impermanence. Things change as quickly and commonly as do the updates on our computer.

It is hard to argue about the unpredictability of our current time. What is easily overlooked in the identification of contemporary life with change is the need all human beings still have to find some sort of permanence and stability in their lives. The external realities may speak of change; internally, I feel it is safe to say that the need for something constant and predictable is deep and basic to the human soul. If we do not find that constancy in other human beings, in our institutions, and in what society values, then we will find those marks of permanence in other, sometimes surprising places.

It is up to wise leaders, as well as adults guiding and mentoring young people, to speak about and steer young people toward healthy signs of permanence and continuity. The change our world is enduring is staggering, and frightening at times to even the wisest and most confident of leaders. How easy it is to gravitate toward whatever we can find that gives us a sense of certainty. This makes the work of identifying and modeling what can be healthy, truly enduring marks of permanence all the more important.

---

*See, "Faculty Motivation, Schedule Change, and School Change," *Ideas and Perspectives*, 39, no. 1, (January 20, 2014), 3.

Getting the Soul Out of Bed

March 31, 2014

The whole secret of the teacher's force lies in the conviction that men are convertible. And they are. They want awakening.

– Ralph Waldo Emerson

There may be no more fashionable word today, in our educational lexicon, than "engagement." When our students respond positively to a particular class or program, we will describe them as being "really engaged." As we strive to build loyalty to and support for our school, we hope our parents and alumnae will feel truly engaged in our community life. Likewise, when there is an absence of involvement, when students seem bored or distant, we will say they're disengaged. If we elect not to get emotionally involved in something, we will say that we "choose not to be engaged." In so many venues, we speak of active, interested, and personal involvement as being engaged.

Clearly, there is something more to the use of this word than simply intellectual curiosity. There is a degree to which the heart, indeed the soul, is involved. Much of one's whole being is alive to the moment, the enterprise: one has become a stakeholder in a very deep way. Like the traditional use of the term engagement, educational engagement has a binding quality to it that transcends academic achievement or intellectual fascination. It is a prelude, hopefully, to something much more: perhaps a lifelong commitment?

Emerson did not commonly use the word, "engagement." He did, however, speak of the process of "getting the soul out of bed, out of her deep sleep," awakening hearts and minds together to the joys and mystery of learning. That was the desire, he claimed, even of secular teachers.

I think that underlines what we look for in engagement: we want the soul to be inspired, to be joined to the mind in the learning process. We want it to begin a journey, and we hope that journey will bind those souls to a love of learning and a sense of loyalty to our schools.

The Reverend Samuel Dewitt Proctor once described a student he taught, who got very good grades but never really invested himself in his work or what the school was seeking to awaken in him. "He went through school," Proctor observed, "but school did not go through him."

That is something of what engagement is all about. As we enter into one of the busiest and most stressful times of the year, it is good to remind ourselves of what we seek for our students. We want their souls to get out of bed. We want school to go through them! What's more, Emerson would say—despite all evidence to the contrary—that those souls are waiting for just that!

It Can Wait

April 7, 2014

You may have heard of AT&T's campaign to eliminate texting while driving, entitled, "It Can Wait." Using dramatic videos featuring stories of what can happen to peoples' lives as a result of a driver texting behind the wheel, the campaign is meant to undermine the false sense of confidence teenagers feel when they text while driving. As the campaign's signature refrain goes, "No text is worth dying for."

The intent behind the program is admirable and compelling, and the stories told by the families of victims as well as by those drivers who caused death or injury can be heart-wrenching. What the campaign seems to lack, however, is a stated rationale for its very title, "It Can Wait." At no point does there seem to be an explanation of what the slogan means. Presumably it is implying that there are some things in life more important than others, and that the less important matters in life, such as texting, can wait.

You might say that our culture is more drawn to the theme, "What are you waiting for?" than, "It can wait." We seem to confuse the capacity to do something—such as texting while driving—with the rightness of doing something, particularly when it causes great danger to others. Because we can do something does not mean that we should do something.

Some things can wait. I know that one of the most vulnerable times in my work is when I open my email account and, seeing a very large number of messages, begin to feel the pressure to respond to those messages quickly and efficiently. It is a vulnerable time because some of those messages would be best responded to, in a calmer and wiser fashion, after some thought and time. Almost always, if I wait rather than immediately respond, I send a more reasoned and gracious response.

Episcopal schools are about trying to determine what can wait and what can't. To be sure, there is much we need to respond to quickly and decisively. But, as Ned Murray, head of Episcopal Day School in Augusta, Georgia, reminds us in a recent TEDx talk he did,* our work as educators is about what matters, and it is a matter of discerning what is truly important at any given time. Modern life comes at us aggressively, expecting from us immediate responses to everything. Our task, including what we need to model for our students and families, is to sort out the important from the urgent, what requires a thoughtful response rather than a hurried response, and in many cases making the courageous decision to wait.

*See, www.youtube.com/watch?v=nQrp4PBhH94.

Going Deeper

April 14, 2014

In his new book, *The Curmudgeon's Guide to Getting Ahead: Do's and Don'ts of Right Behavior, Tough Thinking, Clear Writing, and Living a Good Life*, Charles Murray takes on a number of assumptions that lay claim to holding the key to leading a happy, fulfilling life. One of those assumptions, known well in many schools, is that "smart people don't believe in that religious stuff anymore." Murray himself is an agnostic, but confesses that his "unbelief is getting shaky." Perhaps we haven't "moved beyond" religion as much as we might think. Take religion seriously, he tells us. See what it has to say. "Getting inside the wisdom of the great religions doesn't happen by sitting on beaches, watching sunsets and waiting for enlightenment. It can easily require as much intellectual effort as a law degree."

Getting to the depths of religion, as he has attempted to do, has convinced him that so many of the great religious traditions bear no resemblance to their popular portrayals, be they in the media or in the assumptions of many sophisticated people. Pay no attention, he tells us, to media portrayals of religion, or what many bright people assume to be its irrelevance: what you have gathered or assumed may well be no more than what Thoreau referred to as learning things at second hand. He advises us, "You have got to grapple with the real thing."

"Find ways to put yourself around people who are profoundly religious," he continues. "You will encounter individuals whose intelligence, judgment, and critical faculties are as impressive as those of your smartest atheist friends—and who also possess a disquieting confidence in an underlying reality behind the many religious dogmas."

Admittedly, it is hard to go to the deeper level of almost anything these days. The manner in which we dart from one thing to another—be it with activities or our shortened attention spans—is hardly conducive to serious probing. Still, Holy Week provides us with a unique opportunity to journey beneath the surface of belief, to see the deeper dimensions of faith and its message for a world that hungers for grace and redemption. This we can do in with a community of people who grapple with the mystery unfolding this week We will encounter, in the suffering, death and resurrection of Jesus Christ, not only a pattern that defines Christianity, but a pattern that defines life itself.

Some of our schools will be experiencing Holy Week in chapel and classes. Others are taking the week off, thereby offering us the possibility of time for rest and reflection. Whatever the context, Holy Week extends us an invitation: to go deeper.

Like the Very First Time

April 22, 2014

Last Monday during Holy Week I was privileged to speak at and be a part of the lower school chapel at Saint Andrew's School in Boca Raton, Florida. As part of that service, a group of students from the Christian Fellowship in the lower school re-enacted the events of Jesus' life on Maundy Thursday, as Jesus sat with his disciples in the room upstairs. The students recounted and re-lived the events that led up to and included the Last Supper, and I was astonished, looking out over the student body, how silent the room was, let alone how carefully this large group of students—from pre-kindergarten through fifth grade—watched the unfolding of the story right before them.

It was as if these students were seeing this drama for the very first time. Indeed, it may well be that some of them had never encountered these events before—literally it was their first time to hear and see the story.

I marveled at how they were not only attentive to but almost transfixed on the story, and I thought about how the great events of the Christian story—celebrated this past week and continuing into this Easter season—beckon to us, and invite us to experience them as if for the first time. We have the opportunity not just to remember these events, through which God accomplishes the plan of redemption, but to encounter and experience them all over again, as if we ourselves were that very group of confused, forlorn, and ultimately joyful disciples making that original journey with Jesus.

Once again, in the actions and attitudes of our students, we see an invitation from God offered to us—come experience the story of salvation all over again, as if for the very first time. No wonder we feel so blessed and challenged by being in Episcopal schools!

Skeptics and Cynics

April 28, 2014

This past week I had the opportunity to hear Bethany McLean, a prominent business journalist, speak in Chicago. She has written on both the Enron scandal as well as the financial crisis of 2008. In her talk she made reference to an important distinction—whether it has to do with the business world or even the gospel we might have heard this past Sunday, featuring Doubting Thomas—between a skeptic and a cynic.

The skeptic may well be the one who remains unconvinced, who questions, doubts, and tempers the enthusiasm for a new idea or initiative. Ms. McLean spoke about the skeptic as the one who has the courage to say, "I don't get it," noting how rare it can be in the business world to hear someone willing to say just that. This is the person who takes the risk of being viewed as the outsider, and who may well be seeing things that others do not see.

The cynic is someone who, as one observer put it, "obsesses over what is broken." This is the person who not only holds a dim view of the idea being proposed, but also the capacity of human beings to accomplish it in the first place. Rather than wanting to know more, pressing for a fuller picture of a plan, the cynic tries to make the idea look faulty in the first place. The skeptic inquires, the cynic casts aspersions.

The skeptic can be a real asset to a deliberative discussion, while the cynic can be toxic.

Needless to say, we live in the midst of a good deal of cynicism in our culture, and we can see it alive and well in our schools, whether among young people or adults. How easy it would be, then, to picture Thomas as a cynic, rather than a skeptic. He doesn't immediately accept that the person in front of him, in that room, is the resurrected Christ. But Thomas pushes toward a solution, indeed offers a way out of his own doubt. He asks to put his finger in Jesus' side. The cynic, on the other hand, would be far more likely to walk away from the scene, eager to hold one of those inevitable "meetings after the meeting."

Episcopal schools are places of rigorous inquiry. That is why we welcome the Doubting Thomas, indeed talk of him often in our Easter season chapels. Episcopal schools are also places of commitment and profession; we do not wallow in our negativity. Thomas, like any good skeptic, is capable of being convinced. His ultimate profession ultimately is as strong and robust as any we see in the Bible. In that way he serves as an apt model of all that is powerful and good about our schools.

Consideration

May 5, 2014

Over the years I have come to value greatly the wisdom, pastoral care, and calm focus of Connie Wootton, executive director of the Southwestern Association of Episcopal Schools. A few weeks ago, at a conference on leadership and governance in Dallas, I saw and heard Connie at her very best.

She spoke on the notion of consideration, a word we use often in the daily life of Episcopal schools. However, Connie took that word to a deeper level. Consideration is not simply about "being nice," she reminded us. It is, instead, about giving serious thought to how those with different viewpoints than our own are to be treated, honored, and respected in our schools.

Our schools are blessed with people who feel passionately about what they do. That passion so often carries with it a deep sense of commitment to what is felt to be right. It can also, quite understandably, involve a low tolerance level for those who do not hold the same viewpoint on what is right, let alone do not feel the same investment of heart and soul in the values we so cherish.

Connie reminded us that consideration is the ability—cultivated deliberately—to look upon others as worthy of their point of view, no matter how different that view might be from our own.

This, she reminded us, is an outgrowth of our commitment to the dignity of every human being, in Episcopal schools, as well as the price we pay for believing that every single person's view merits such worth. To be places of welcome and hospitality, Episcopal schools are about making room for disparate points of view.

To be sure, nothing is harder than embracing this form of consideration. What's more, nothing could be more challenging during these intense spring weeks leading up to the conclusion of the school year.

As Connie wisely reminded us, speaking of that person whose viewpoint is so different, seemingly so foreign to our own, "He or she is not there by chance." Rather than attempting to bring that person around to our own point of view, perhaps the essence of consideration is about taking the time to try and understand that differing point of view, and then wondering why God has put that person on our path, in this community, in the first place.

Communities of Trust

May 12, 2014

This past week I had the privilege of being at a middle school chapel at St. Matthew's Episcopal Day School in San Mateo, California. There I heard the head of school, Mark McKee, give a talk about the role of trust in our individual and collective lives. At one point he asked some of the middle school students what their definitions of trust were. One student responded that trust is about the belief that the other person has your best interests in mind. Mark added one of his own definitions: the assumption that you and the other person will keep your word.

This substantive discussion on trust reminded me of an essay that former secretary of state, Warren Christopher, wrote in the first volume of the series, *This I Believe*. You may be familiar with that series on National Public Radio. In that article Christopher recalled an evening when he was driving down a two-lane highway. As another automobile approached from the opposite direction, traveling at the same speed and eventually passing by his car, Christopher thought about just how much he was relying on that other driver not to swerve into his lane, to be distracted by a cell phone conversation, or to fall asleep at the wheel. So, too, that driver was relying on Christopher to do the same. All of this led him to conclude:

Multiplied a million times over, I believe this is the way the world works. At some level, we all depend upon one another. Sometimes that dependence requires us simply to refrain from doing something, like crossing over a yellow line. And sometimes it requires us to act cooperatively, with allies or even with strangers.

We might add to that list: with members of our school community.

So much of our daily life in schools is based on trust, and how that element of trust can get tested this time of year. Whether or not our schools have honor codes, we go about our lives unconsciously assuming that we and the other people we interact with are keeping our word, or, as Christopher put it, relying on "the good faith and judgment of others."

In his talk with the students, Mark McKee reminded them that this spirit of trust begins with us, and our ability to be trustworthy.

At this time of year, when things seem as if they are on autopilot, it may sound trite to remind ourselves of these fundamental notions of trust. Something tells me, however, that those notions are at the root of how we make our way through these days!

Being Watched

May 19, 2014

In Simon Blackburn's new book, *Mirror, Mirror: The Uses and Abuses of Self-Love*, the story is told of an experiment once done by a member of the psychology department at Newcastle University in England. In the department's communal lounge, where faculty and staff could get coffee and tea, an honor system was in place: one was expected to pay for the coffee and tea used by putting money into a collection box. The department was finding, however, that the collection always was coming up short; clearly someone was not paying their share of the coffee and tea being used.

A member of the department decided it was time for a behavioral experiment. For the next few weeks a frieze of flowers was placed above the notice reminding people of the system and the costs for beverages consumed. No significant change was seen in the amount of money collected. Then a picture of a human face was posted, replacing the frieze, with a man looking directly at the consumer. During the weeks the face was posted, the collection box yielded three times the amount of money as had been gathered during the previous weeks! Blackburn concluded that our awareness of being watched, even in a symbolic fashion, makes a difference in our behavior.

Our hope for our students is that they will do the right thing, in whatever circumstance, because they sincerely wish to do the right thing. Character, as one writer defines it, is about what we do when no one is watching. We seek to instill in our students an intrinsic, internally-driven motivation to do right, rather than out of fear of being caught or punished. Blackburn's example of the Newcastle experiment, however, tells us that the presence of other people, and their potential observations of our behavior, continues to be an important factor in what we do in given circumstances in our lives.

I think of two important implications for the reality that "being watched" influences our adult behavior in schools. The first is that we need to be present among our students, graciously but intentionally watching them. Children and teenagers rely upon that important adult presence, including the watchful eye, far more than we might at first realize. The second is that the same goes for all of us as adults: we are being watched by our students for clues on how adult life is to be lived. Indeed, the realization that adult life is about, as I am fond of identifying it, the activity of being watched, can be a useful reminder to us of the importance of responsible behavior and moral seriousness in our work with young people.

The End of Vacation?

June 2, 2014

Given how much I travel in my work, it will come as no surprise to hear that I am often a "compulsory eavesdropper" on telephone conversations in airport terminals or on airplanes. One afternoon, recently, the gentleman in the seat behind me was having a telephone conversation that I could not help but hear. He was describing an employment opportunity in his firm, no doubt to a potential applicant for the position. He got around to talking about benefits, and specifically the number of vacation days initially allotted to the successful candidate. After identifying a particular number of days, he quickly added, "Of course there is no such thing as vacation anymore."

I catalogued his comment into the "sweeping statement" category of comments I have heard or read this past year, including, "No one has time for anything, anymore," and, "There are no heroes anymore."

Sweeping statements they may be, but each one compels our attention by virtue of their—at the very least—bordering on truth.

As we conclude the school year, wishing each other a happy summer vacation and anticipating a change of pace in our lives, I would ask if that employer's sweeping generalization may well be true: is there no such thing as vacation anymore? Having seen many people in recent years supposedly on vacation but dutifully plugged in to work, do we now face the prospect of a "vacationless" summer? Is it logistically impossible? Are we able to function apart from our work, or at least those parts of work that pop up on our devices while we are physically away from work? Do we have the capacity to disengage, or have we lost a freedom that we may have once possessed?

Here is my challenge for the summer ahead: prove that employer to be wrong. While I do not envy the person on the other end of the phone that may have him for a boss, I don't render his pronouncement an inevitability. If for no other reason, we owe it to our students and colleagues to return to school in August or September having been renewed, perhaps even having spent some time away from the things that plug us in to life each day during the school year. Indeed, many of our students will return to us tired and stressed out from the summer months; they do not need an adult reflecting back to them that "vacationless" feeling.

Is there no such thing as vacation anymore? It is up to us to answer that question!

About Daniel R. Heischman

The Reverend Daniel R. Heischman, D.D., executive director of the National Association of Episcopal Schools (NAES), began his tenure on July 1, 2007. Prior to his work with NAES, Mr. Heischman was College Chaplain at Trinity College, Hartford, Connecticut, for four years. He was head of the upper school and assistant headmaster of St. Albans School, Washington, DC, from 1994 through 2003. From 1987 to 1994 he was executive director of the Council for Religion in Independent Schools (CRIS), now the Center for Spiritual and Ethical Education (CSEE). He served as chaplain and then assistant headmaster of Trinity School, New York, New York, from 1979 until 1987. He began his ordained ministry in 1976 at St. Paul's Episcopal Church, Englewood, New Jersey.

A noted speaker, workshop leader, and author, Mr. Heischman is an instructor in doctor of ministry studies at Virginia Theological Seminary, Alexandria, Virginia. He preaches and leads faculty and parent workshops and retreats at Episcopal and independent schools, and serves as a facilitator for faculty development programs related to ethics and the moral development of students. His most recent publications are the books, *Good Influence: Teaching the Wisdom of Adulthood* (New York, NY: Morehouse

Publishing, 2009) and *What Schools Teach Us about Religious Life* (New York, NY: Peter Lang, 2014). He has also contributed articles to the *Journal of Religion and Health, The Christian Century,* and numerous school bulletins and publications.

The 2006 recipient of NAES' John D. Verdery Award for outstanding service to Episcopal schools and the Association, Mr. Heischman served as a member (1995-2001) and treasurer (1996-2001) of the NAES Governing Board. He has also served on the boards of the Association of Independent Maryland Schools (AIMS); the Religious Education Association; Berkeley Divinity School at Yale, and a number of independent and Episcopal schools. He is currently president of the board of the Council for American Private Education, an association of private school organizations of which NAES is a founding member.

Mr. Heischman was educated at the College of Wooster in Wooster, Ohio, where he earned a bachelor of arts degree, Phi Beta Kappa, in 1973. He attended Jesus College, University of Cambridge in the United Kingdom, earning a bachelor of arts degree in theology in 1975 and a master of arts degree in 1978. He earned a master of sacred theology degree from Yale Divinity School, New Haven, Connecticut in 1976, and in 1987 he earned a doctor of ministry degree from Princeton Theological Seminary in Princeton, New Jersey. He received a doctor of divinity degree, *honoris causa*, from Berkeley Divinity School at Yale, New Haven, Connecticut in 2011 in recognition of his many years of distinguished service to Episcopal schools and universities.